# *A Shephard's Soul*

## A Letter to You:

Before you turn this page, I want you to pause for a moment.

This book was not written by accident. It was written through prayer, pressure, growth, and obedience. Every page carries lessons learned in quiet rooms, in difficult seasons, and in moments when faith had to be stronger than fear.

You are holding more than words. You are holding intention.

My hope is that somewhere within these pages, you find confirmation that your story matters, your calling is real, and your journey is not random. If you feel stretched, you are growing. If you feel challenged, you are being refined. If you feel unseen, know that purpose often develops in private before it is revealed in public.

This book is an invitation.

An invitation to build with vision.

To lead with heart.

To stand firm when it would be easier to fold.

To shepherd what has been entrusted to you — your family, your vision, your legacy.

If even one sentence strengthens you, challenges you, or shifts your perspective, then these pages have done their job.

Thank you for trusting me with your time. Thank you for allowing these words into your space.

Now let's build something that outlives us.

With purpose,

Andre' Shephard Jr.

## Table of Contents

**Chapter 1 — Shackled to Misery**
Tormented by grief, guilt, and unresolved trauma, Andre spirals into addiction and sleepless nights, resisting the help that could save him.

**Chapter 2 — Forced Forward**
Pulled toward help against his will, Andre confronts anxiety, addiction, and the reality that his freedom, family, and future hang in the balance.

**Chapter 3 — The Run-In**
At the height of his popularity and confidence, Andre's need for attention and dominance sets the stage for choices that quietly follow him into adulthood.

**Chapter 4 — Help is on the Way**
As therapy turns personal, Andre confronts buried trauma, shared loss, and faith itself, discovering that healing begins when he finally allows himself to be seen.

**Chapter 5 — Crossroads**
Andre's world shifts when his mother announces her engagement to Manny, a man he distrusts. Tensions erupt at home as Dre grapples with loyalty, fear, and the harsh realities of adulthood colliding with the innocence of childhood.

**Chapter 6 — Calamity Calls**
Manny's abuse escalates, forcing Andre and his mother to survive growing danger. When Tay and Teela announce their pregnancies, Dre confronts responsibility, fear, and guilt, while his mother takes decisive steps to protect her children.

**Chapter 7 — F.O.E. (Friends Over Everything)**
Amidst trauma and instability, Andre finds refuge in friendship and faith. His bond with Zion strengthens as they navigate

mischief, arrests, and survival, learning resilience, loyalty, and the unexpected presence of God.

## Chapter 8 — Uprooting

After being forced from their home, Andre and Zion face survival, strained relationships, and past trauma. Through adversity, they discover adaptability, loyalty, and the choices that shape a more stable future.

## Chapter 9 — Turning Point

A shooting lands Andre in jail and puts Zion in danger. Battling guilt, probation, and love drama, Dre leans on God and loyal friends to navigate life's shifting loyalties and challenges.

## Chapter 10 — Lost in the Shuffle

Dre loses Zion in a tragic fight. Holding him as he bleeds, Andre faces heartbreak, guilt, and the harsh reality that the streets have no forgiveness.

## Chapter 11 — The Seed

Amid grief and loss, Andre begins to learn resilience. Life presses forward, demanding that he rise above or be consumed by it.

## Chapter 12 — Mercy

Facing a prison sentence, Andre experiences God's mercy and his family's unwavering support, igniting hope for a better tomorrow.

## Chapter 13 — Chains and Choices

Andre navigates his first months in prison, confronting survival, faith, and the pull of his past, while wrestling with family ties and the weight of loss.

## Chapter 14 — Faith in the Fire

A spiritual awakening reshapes Andre's heart. From transformative experiences in the faith-based dorm to family reunions and tests of release, this chapter explores redemption, forgiveness, and the power of God to turn broken circumstances into purpose.

## Present Day — A Shephard's Rhodes

A Glimpse into a Life Restored: Andre Celebrates Peace, Joy, and a Growing Family. Surrounded by answered prayers and blessings, he reflects on God's faithfulness, setting the stage for the next chapter in *A Shephard's Rhodes*.

## *Acknowledgments*

First and foremost, I give all honor and glory to God. Thank You for never leaving me nor forsaking me. Even when I doubted myself, You were faithful. I hold firmly to this truth: He who has begun a good work in you will carry it on to completion until the day of Jesus Christ. Every trial, every hardship, every breaking season was not wasted. I am grateful for the tribulations, for through them You were shaping me for Your glory, as reminded in Ephesians 3:13. What once felt like pain became purpose.

Secondly, I thank my mother. No matter how hard I made things, no matter how far I strayed or how much resistance I gave, you never stopped loving me. Your unwavering support and sacrifice carried me through more than you'll ever know. Most importantly, thank you for making sure we knew the Truth—Jesus Christ. That foundation is the reason I am still standing.

To my big brother—thank you for being more than a brother. You stepped into the role of a father when you didn't have to. You carried burdens that were never meant to be yours, yet you did it with strength, patience, and love. I am forever grateful for your presence and protection in my life.

To Zion—thank you for guarding me during seasons when I made reckless decisions and didn't listen. You stood watch even when I ignored wisdom. It took nearly twenty years to forgive myself, and though the pain still lingers, I acknowledge your role in keeping me alive long enough to heal.

And finally, my greatest earthly blessing—my wife. You are my safe place. Thank you for staying up late, editing page after page, pushing me when I wanted to quit, and calling me to higher standards when I settled for less. Thank you for your patience with my stubbornness, but more than that, thank you for helping me confront my past and walking every painful step with me. This

book exists because you believed in me before I fully believed in myself.

This work is more than words on pages—it is a testimony. And to everyone who played a role, seen or unseen, thank you. God is not finished with me yet.

# 1. Shackled To Misery!

*"Come unto me, all ye that labour and are heavy laden, and I will give you rest."* **— Matthew 11:28—**

Heart pounding, body trembling, eyes raining with tears as I registered the words that will forever haunt me.

"NO! I DON'T BELIEVE YOU!" I screamed with every hope that the news I just received wasn't true. The detective stood there with empathy in his eyes, witnessing something so familiar, yet it never got any easier.

"I'm so, so sorry, baby," the sweet apologetic voice cried through the phone—attempting to caress my broken soul.

"WHYYYYY GOD? WHY? I'M SO SORRY, BRO! I PRAYED! WHY DIDN'T YOU ANSWER?" I questioned God as an invisible coal formed in the back of my throat, making it hard to swallow. A thunderstorm of tears continued to precipitate, but with greater force as my soul wept with guilt. My stomach felt like my organs were tying into one big knot.

"ANDRE! ANDRE!" A voice cried out in rescue, "Andre, wake up, baby!"

Sinking into my darkness, I mustered up the last bit of strength to open my eyes. I was relieved to see my wife.

"Tam! It happened again!" I said, discouraged as I slumped into her warm, loving embrace. She wrapped her arms around me—comforting me like a mother holding her child who was startled by a nightmare.

"Baby, you need to get help. You've been having these nightmares since that day," she pleaded, once again trying to convince me to go to the MHMR clinic.

"Bae, what did I tell you?" I pushed her off me, frustrated with the pressure from everyone advising me to get "*help*," as they called it. I know my wife is concerned, but from what I've heard about MHMR, I refused to check it out myself.

"Love, if I go…."

"It'll just make things worse," she mocked, knowing exactly what I was going to say. "But baby, this has been happening since—" she caught herself. Hoping to prevent any more damage to my fragile heart, she said, "I'll go with you. You can't just keep smoking, thinking that's the cure. For one, you are on probation, and two, that doesn't really help you. And don't even start," Tam said, putting her foot down. Clearly, she was tired of this same conversation, like a rerun on B.E.T.

"I know you're right, but I'm scared," I said in my defense. *No way on earth could she convince me to go to the nut house,* as I liked to call it.

"Do it for me," she pleaded, staring at me with tears of love. "I hate seeing you crying in your sleep. That is the saddest thing I've ever seen, baby."

"Ugh, ok, I'll go, but it's only for you! If I don't like it, I'm going to continue to smoke, because Mary Jane understands me," I answered. She rolled her eyes as if I said something stupid, but I had it all figured out. Nothing was going to stop me from smoking, so I decided I would just go to appease her and then say I didn't like it.

"Good, I have an appointment set up for you for tomorrow," she said, quickly rolling over and pretending to be asleep like a child who knew they were in trouble.

"Wait! What? An APPOINTMENT?" I raised my voice in anger, yet silence filled the room. It was so quiet you could hear the doorbell ring from three units down.

"Hello? So, I'm talking to myself now?" I asked rhetorically, looking for a reaction from my wife, but she refused to budge. "Ok, you're right! Doing shady shit behind my back!" I said, knowingly provoking an argument. Before I could fully calm down, I heard the masculine voice speak out loud, "That's why I'm not going!"

I immediately had a flashback of my mother lecturing me, *"Son, if you don't have anything nice to say, then keep your thoughts to yourself."* Clearly, history repeats itself, because like before, I didn't listen.

Tam shot up like a firecracker on the fourth of July. She had a familiar look on her face that every husband has surely seen. That *"oh really? That's yo ass!"* look.

"You're not doing what?" her voice echoed, filling the room as if she were speaking through an intercom.

"Oh, well, hello there. Now you can hear me. Look at God! Won't he do it!" I replied with sarcasm; positive, I pissed her off this time.

"You promised Dre. SEE! I knew you were going to do this," she whined, before starting the reverse psychology that only women knew how to do best. "Well, fine! Guess I'll just stay mad at you until you go then," she stated as she rolled over. "Enjoy the silent treatment."

I laid there thinking about the silent treatment and how unfair the punishment was, *like c'mon. Really, you're not going to talk to me at all? My God, the childishness; the pettiness! I hate it when she wins.*

"Ok, Tam, I'll go," I gave in.

She rolled back over and hugged me. "Thank you, babe! I love you so much. I promise, I just want you to get better," she said as she kissed me. Her lips were soft and moist, sparking a tingle that rushed through my body, reaching my cold heart.

"I love you too," I replied as she snuggled up against me, drifting off to sleep.

As Tam laid peacefully in my arms, I found comfort in the warmth of her thick chocolate shape. Yet, I could not ease myself back to sleep—fearing my nightmare would come back and finish breaking the rest of my heart. Staring at the ceiling, I started thinking about the worst day of my life. "It's all my fault," I whispered to myself as my eyes began to flood. I had so many unanswered questions, but the main one was *WHY? Why did I have to show off? Why didn't I listen to anybody? Why couldn't I have just let it go?!* The guilt began to consume me, and my head started to hurt. *I can't take this anymore. I need to smoke,* I thought. I slid my arm from under my wife and grabbed my weed and swishers, as I headed outside to smoke my pain away. When I approached the mirror by the stairs, I stopped, not recognizing the man staring back at me. Nappy hair, unkept beard, a bloated gut, not to mention the musty stench; it was clear I had let myself go since that night.

I stood there staring at myself in disgust, damn *when was the last time you bathed? Ever since that day, you went from a light-skinned, pretty boy with an athletic body, to an ugly, smelly man so out of shape that walking up and down the stairs makes you exhausted. You stopped caring about your responsibilities, your probation, your family, and friends. Ever since that day, you've been walking around like you're the dead man, refusing to forgive yourself and accepting the second chance God gave you! You hate your life, you question God, you carry around a burden that's not even yours to bear. HE'S GONE DRE! He's never coming back. It's time to move on! Don't continue to torment yourself.* I closed my eyes, trying to block the tears from pouring out, but when I opened them, all my emotions came rushing in like a tidal wave.

Since I wasn't allowed to smoke inside the apartment, I went outside and sat on the porch. I was comforted by the coziness of the night. *I wish it were like this all day,* I thought as I started to break down one of the five swishers.

"Man, you taught me everything I know," I said aloud, reflecting on who it was that showed me how to roll a blunt. I gazed at the fireflies that lit up the night sky, feeling one stare back at me. In what had to have been the fastest record in stoner history, I rolled a blunt in under a minute. Impressed by how perfectly rolled the blunt was, I took the lighter and lit the end. I deeply inhaled the smoke, filling my lungs to their capacity. The deeper I inhaled, the more the pain began to fade. I focused back on the night sky, "I'd do anything in the world to take your place."

After a few minutes of staring off into the stars, I finally got up and went back inside. A hunger came out of nowhere like I hadn't eaten in days, or in other words, I had the munchies. Although I was too lazy to make anything, it seems like I never had the energy to cook anymore. In fact, many of the things I used to enjoy doing, I no longer do. After grabbing the biggest bowl I could find, I walked to the cereal cabinet and made a life-changing decision between Lucky Charms and Fruity Pebbles. Next, I got the whole milk from the fridge and listened to the crackles of the Fruity Pebbles as the milk filled the bowl. Taking my midnight snack into the living room, I decided to play Call of Duty on my PlayStation. I turned the TV on and was startled by the loud blast from the surround sound speakers. Trying not to panic, I quickly located the remote to avoid waking my family, but it was too late. A loud cry overpowered the speakers that someone forgot to turn down; that someone being me.

"UGGGGHHHHHHH!" Followed by the loud smack of Tam's lips, let me know she was upset.

"SORRY!" I yelled, apologizing for waking up our 8-month-old son.

"Now come put him back to sleep," she demanded. There was a familiar tone in her voice; tiredness mixed with frustration of the same old same old.

"I'm a little busy at the moment! I'm eating and playing the game," I fired back in between bites. After finishing my cereal, I slurped the milk. That was my favorite part and exactly why I always go for the biggest bowl. The bigger the bowl, the more of the sweet sugary milky goodness.

"You better not be eating out of the big bowl again, and you better clean up after yourself! I'm your wife, not your damn maid!" Tam shouted what every wife has surely told their husband at least once. My wife either knew me too well, or maybe I am predictable and always do the same things. Loud thumps soon walked across the ceiling, indicating her anger as she put our son back to sleep.

With the help of the loud explosions blasting through my headphones, I continued my mission on Call of Duty while I ignored Tam's little attitude. After playing for a while, I noticed how quickly the pain of my memory resurfaced. *Maybe smoking doesn't help*, I thought. *I'll just roll more so that it takes longer for the pain to return.* I had it all figured out; the calculations felt right, and nobody could tell me a thing. *Hell, because at this point, I'd drink a bottle of bleach if it helped take the pain away forever*, I sadly thought.

I walked outside, back to the same spot as before, and started rolling the rest of my weed. Sitting in deep thought, I reflected on how fucked up my life had become. By the time I started rolling the third blunt, my little brother Toni walked up. I was the second oldest of my mother's six kids, and Toni was two years younger than me, but he was bigger than both my older brother Jay and I. He was 5'9 a half, but that extra half stood out, which is why everyone would call him the "Little BIG brother." Besides being taller, he was also more well-rounded than we were in the physical sense, if you know what I mean. I wouldn't quite say he was fat, maybe "big boned." While he was a true teddy bear at heart, he could transform into a Grizzly bear if you poked at him. Toni and I are a lot alike; we both bend the rules, whereas Jay is more on the straight and narrow.

"Can't sleep again?" Toni asked as he sat down next to me.

"You know how I am," I replied nonchalantly.

"Wanna match a blunt?" he offered as he pulled out two nicely rolled blunts. *Of course, it wasn't better than mine.* It was always a competition between us.

"Is water wet?" I asked rhetorically.

*Six blunts! So now that means it's going to take six times longer for the pain to resurface,* I thought. I lit my blunt first and held in the smoke as long as I could until I was ready to release all the built-up stress inside.

"I decided to go get help," I said, trying to break the silence. "What do you think?" I asked, hoping to get some encouragement from my brother.

"You want the truth, or do you want me to make you feel good?" Toni asked in consideration of my feelings.

"I want the truth! Come on, you're my brother," I said seriously.

"Okay, I love you, but yes, you need some type of help. I have never seen you like this before. The only reason I'm sitting here next to your funky ass now is that you're my brother, but you stink. Your clothes don't match, you barely take care of yourself, and on top of all of that, you don't sleep. Hell, if it weren't for weed, I think you would probably starve because you barely eat," my brother openly expressed. "I know you're scared but just think for a second. Remember how popular you were?" he paused as he inhaled the blunt. "You stayed clean! You were OCD about matching your clothes, and we used to damn near have to slap you to wake you up. I know what happened was tragic, but you took it the worst, and we all are worried about you," he finished as a tear fell from his eye like a drip from a faucet.

While I appreciated him being honest, we all know what they say, *"You can't handle the truth!"* My insides felt overwhelmed with pain as if there were a midget using my organs for a punching bag.

"I know, bro, and that's what hurts. I just can't get the vision out of my head," I confessed as the weather forecast from my eyes predicted a slight chance of rain. "I gave up on life. Now, smoking is the only thing that helps me. I hate my life! On top of all that, my innocent wife has to endure all my bullshit—suffering from things that have nothing to do with her. That's why I told her I'd go. For her!" I said, sniffling in a glob of snot.

It was an emotional moment that rarely happens because I hardly see my brother let down his macho side to cry. Nobody said a word; we just sat deep in thought, chain-smoking through three of the six blunts. Finally, after wiping away a tear, my brother looked at me sincerely and said, "No matter how much you change, I will always love you and be here for you. Not exactly sure how, but I'm going to help you, even if it means my last breath." Those words rushed through my body, igniting a surge of warmth. The emotional weather forecast changed from rain to sunny when he said, "Just remember me when you start receiving those checks!"

A loud burst of laughter spewed uncontrollably at the thought of me receiving S.S.I. checks, or what we called a 'crazy check.' "Thank you, bro. You seem to always be there when I need you," I paused as I took another drag of the blunt. "But I really do need to stop smoking," I confessed as I stared at the blunt in my hand. Suddenly, I thought, boy, if my wife had just heard me say that. I can hear her now, oh, that sounds familiar, wonder who else thought of that? Oh yeah, me!'

'Well, first off, I love you too, and that's what I'm here for. Secondly, since you want to stop smoking, that means you don't need the rest of these blunts," he said with a mischievous grin.

"Haha, you're funny. Nice try, Smart Guy; I meant after these three!"

"Can't blame a brother for trying," he joked.

"Where's Jay?" I asked in fear of my older brother walking around the corner, catching me smoking.

"Man, you're tripping! Light the other blunts," Toni demanded.

"Ok." I looked around once more, making sure Jay wasn't in sight.

"Don't worry, he's at home making beats. We're good! You know how he is when he's in the zone," Toni assured.

My older brother Jay didn't like me smoking. In fact, I recall many times him reminding me, "If I catch you smoking again, I'm gonna be all on yo ass like flies on shit."

Thinking about it, I know he was only looking out for me because he wanted me to avoid going to prison. He was just doing his big-brother due diligence, since he's always been the closest thing I had to a father figure. Besides being older, he was also stronger than me. The crazy thing is, I never knew when he had the time to work out, but I swear every time I see him, he looks more buff. On top of that, he was in the Army, so no way in hell did I want to test him and be put in one of those submission holds he learned. I've already seen him punch a guy in his head so hard that it had to have been ringing for weeks. Luckily, he pretty much keeps to himself these days.

Jay is what I call a workaholic because he's very dedicated to his music. Often, he would say, "Music is my job, but the difference between my job and yours is you work 9 to 5, whereas I work 24/7 plus overtime." So, the fact that Toni confirmed he was occupied making beats was great, because when he's making beats, he wouldn't pause even if the house were on fire. I mean, this dude would literally look at the flame, hit save, take out the hard drive, wrap it up for safety, and then try to escape.

As I lit the fourth blunt, I took one of the deepest inhales I've ever taken until I could no longer hold in the potency. My lungs deflated—exhaling out a cloud of smoke like a train going full speed. Coughing, choking, with my eyes tearing up, my brother pounded on my back, attempting to help me catch my breath.

"Easy, young buck. That must be my Dro," he said, laughing. He had Hydroponic, also known as Dro, a highly expensive weed grown with a specific technique that uses a lot of water and no soil to increase quality and potency. All I had was "Corn," a less expensive batch with quality somewhere between Dro and "Reggie," also known as regular weed. You see, I'm a Street

Weedologist; I studied weed, I grew weed, I smoked weed, and I lived weed.

"Man, this is some good shit," I said, gasping in between puffs.

"When do you have to take your next drug test?" Toni asked in concern.

"I forgot," I replied. "But I know it's not for another couple of weeks," I was finally able to muster out the lie once I got my wind back.

"That's what you said last time and come to find out it was the next day!" Toni fact-checked me.

I inhaled the blunt again, lightly this time, as a person who only smokes to look cool does. I blew a fog of smoke into my brother's face, "Don't worry, I got this."

"Alright, bro. You always say that, but you need to get serious about stopping. Ten years of probation ain't no joke and I ain't trying to scream free NiggaMan," he stated as I passed him the blunt. "I only smoke with you because I'd rather see you do this than kill yourself because you can't handle life anymore," Toni uttered.

"I know, but it's going to be ok. Trust me. I'm going to go get help tomorrow, and I'm gonna stop smoking for real this time." Although I sounded confident, for some reason, it felt like Déjà vu.

"Okay, I'm just making sure nothing happens to you because you've said that like 17 times now, but who's counting?" Amid Toni's sarcasm, I felt genuine love and concern for my well-being. By the time we finished the fourth blunt, I was ready to tap out, so I told Toni to save the other two for later. We shook hands as we went our separate ways. I loved that we all had our own apartments in the same complex; it made life easier when one of us needed something.

"I love you, bro," he yelled out as he walked down the narrow sidewalk leading to his apartment.

"I love you more!" I replied as I walked back into the security of my home. Inside these walls, no one could hurt me, no one could judge me, no one could provoke me with untruths; no one except me. Just as I started to feel a little better, my mind began to scramble again with painful thoughts. LIES! I RAN? ARE YOU FUCKING KIDDING ME? I walked into the living room to shut everything down because I was too high and too tormented again to do anything. All I needed at this point was sleep. I tiptoed up the stairs—opening the door, sliding into bed like a teenager sneaking back in. I kissed my wife's forehead and gently put my arm around her, trying not to wake the sleeping bear as I fell into my own deep hibernation.

## <u>2. Forced Forward</u>

*"The steps of a good man are ordered by the Lord: and he delighteth in his way."*
— **Psalm 37:23—**

Tossing in my torments, my vision began to focus in, as my wife repeatedly shook me, "Andre, wake up!"

"I don't wanna get up," I whined.

"Andre, you promised me, SO GET UP NOW!" she demanded.

I opened my eyes to the sight of a 20-pound baby drooling and staring at me. Even though I didn't give him my DNA, I gave him my heart. He was never a step to me—he was my son in every way that truly matters.

Looking at my alarm clock, I noticed it said 10 AM. Before I could say anything, my son crawled over, climbed on top of me, and started slapping my face.

"Okay, I give up. I give up, Zion,' I said, surrendering to my son's abusive behavior. W*onder who he gets this from*, I thought, staring at his mom. "Good morning to you, too, Big Noodle. Daddy owes someone a knuckle sandwich," I joked as I tickled him—making him laugh in the cutest baby chuckle.

"You were helping Mama, weren't you, Big Noodle?" Tam said as she handed me a plate of eggs, bacon, pancakes, biscuits, a bowl of steaming hot grits, and a cold glass of milk.

*This looks like a 90s breakfast commercial,* I thought. "I knew I smelled something burning," I joked before I started inhaling the food.

"Real funny, but how many times have you seen me burn anything since you met me?" she asked confidently. "Anyways, you need to hurry up because you stink and you need to shower," she ordered as she grabbed Big Noodle. "But someone is taking one first. Say daddy I stink, but you win the award for the smelliest," she imitated a baby voice.

"I wouldn't quit my day job to pursue comedy if I were you," I said, taking a quick whiff of myself. There was no doubt I stunk, but even with the strong musty odor, the sweet, delicious aroma of the food overpowered my funk. I grabbed my fork and kept feasting. I had already finished the warm, fluffy pancakes with the sweet syrup and creamy butter that melted in my mouth like cotton candy. Next, I devoured the homemade bacon and egg biscuit sandwich I had perfectly crafted. Last was my favorite, buttery grits with sugar. I literally drank the grits and washed it all down with a cold glass of milk.

"Wow! Did you even chew?" my wife asked in shock, as she returned with a freshly bathed baby in his birthday suit. "Shower is all yours, Stank," she said, calling me by the nickname she knew I hated.

"How about you pick out my clothes?" I said, unamused, before heading towards the bathroom with my socks and boxers.

"Don't I always? I swear, sometimes it feels like I have two kids instead of one. What would you do without me?" Tam asked a woman's favorite question.

"Probably kill myself," I answered honestly. *Anything is better than living at this point*, I thought.

"Dre, what did I tell you about talking like that, and especially in front of my son? I don't even know why you say those things. You should be happy that you're still" She quickly stopped herself. Even though she didn't finish, I knew exactly what she was about to say. She walked towards me, noticing the tears forming, and said, "Stank, just forget what I was saying and go take your shower." I knew my wife never meant to hurt me, but being around me was like walking on eggshells. "Come here, babe, I'm sorry," she said as she kissed my cheek.

"I know," I nodded, feeling hopeless. It's all my fault, I thought. Before I could get sucked back into sorrow, I felt something grab my leg. I looked down and saw a joyful smile from

Big Noodle, his arms outstretched, indicating he wanted some love too. "Aw, you want a hug?" I asked as I picked him up. "Mama didn't put a diaper on you, so don't." I stopped mid-sentence as he did exactly what I was thinking. He peed all over me and laughed, as if this were a joke. "I love you too," I said as I handed him over to my wife and went to take my shower.

I walked into the bathroom and turned on the hot water. After getting undressed, I stepped into the tub, and instantly my mind began racing over the "help" I was about to receive. As I stood there, anchored by my own thoughts and the hot water showering down my body, a part of me wondered whether therapy would do more harm than good.

"Baby, your clothes are on the counter. Now, please hurry. Your appointment is in 45 minutes, but it takes about 30 minutes to get there." My wife's words dragged me back into reality. I quickly washed up and got out as instructed. After getting dressed, I walked into the room, ready to go. "Now all you have to do is shave and do something with your hair, so you look like the man I fell in love with," Tam said, trying to ignite a flame of self-confidence.

"Yeah, yeah, whatever. You ready?" I said dismissively as I walked towards the door.

"Yeah, we're ready," she said as she zipped up the baby bag.

I picked up Zion and strapped him into his car seat while directing my wife to turn off all the lights, grab the baby bottles, close the windows, and lock the door. I then walked down the stairs behind her, like the gentleman my mother raised. When we got to the sidewalk, I started feeling more nervous. *I don't want to go, but then again, I know I can't keep feeling like this.* As we approached my 1993 Dodge Spirit, I got the feeling that I was forgetting something, but I didn't know what. I unlocked the doors and secured Zion before getting in the driver's seat. When I started the car, the speakers instantly blasted, startling the baby.

"Really? Why do I always have to repeat everything? What did I tell you about leaving the music up so loud?" Tam scolded, as she hopped in and turned the volume down.

It all seemed like déjà vu. It wasn't until we passed through the main gate that I realized what I left behind. *FUCK! My weed! How could I forget that?* I thought.

"Bae, we have to turn around!"

"Nope. I knew you were going to say that! Let me guess, you forgot your weed?" she replied sarcastically.

I couldn't tell her that, so I thought of a quick lie. "No. I forgot my I.D. So, we definitely have to turn around now." I thought that surely would convince her.

"Nice try, but don't worry, I got it!" She clearly anticipated my shenanigans.

*Damn. I'm out of luck,* I thought. Until I remembered the half-blunt, I had in my secret hiding spot. I decided to wait before pulling it out because I didn't want to hear Tam's mouth.

"Man, I hope traffic isn't bad," I broke the silence to change subjects.

"Yeah, me too," she replied.

**LUB DUB, LUB DUB**, the sound of my heart beating aggressively through my chest. **Don't do it, Dre!** The cry of wisdom from the Holy Spirit in me. **Don't do it, Dre!** The warning from my future wife. **Why Dre? Look at what you've done!** A mixture of my voice and the unforgettable voice that's trapped in my head and tied to my soul cried out.

My eyes began to flood with pain and grief. "I'm sorry, I'm so sorry." I wept like a mother who lost her child, as the pain from the past and present collided—causing havoc.

"BAE!!" Tam screamed, taking me out of my haunted thoughts.

As my vision faded back in, I realized I was approaching a red light. I quickly slammed on the brakes, nearly rear-ending the car in front of me.

"Do you need me to drive?" Tam asked with a mix of sarcasm and concern, before adding, "Because I would love to see tomorrow! Like, for real, are you okay? Sometimes I wish I knew what goes on in your head so I could help you."

"There are millions of thoughts that run through my mind, and trying to chase down one for us to conquer doesn't change nor help the other million that will pop back up."

For my family's safety, I pulled over and let my wife drive the rest of the way. While she sang along to the music, I sat in the passenger seat, staring into the crisp blue sky. I was rescued from my thoughts when my wife grabbed my hand and said, "I love you, and I will always be here for you. We are going to get through this together. Till death do us part, right?" She winked at me.

"Right," I confirmed, allowing her words to comfort me. I spent the rest of the car ride in silence while my wife drove us safely to our destination.

"We're here," Tam announced.

"Good, I need to smoke!" I said as I revealed the hidden blunt. I grabbed my lighter and turned to my wife, "You got everything right?"

"Are you fucking kidding me?" Tam said in her angry, whispering voice, as if we were in public. "You seriously can't wait until after your first therapy session? On top of that, you really think it's okay for me to carry the baby, the stroller, and this big-ass diaper bag so you can get high? Be for real!"

"It'll help me open up," I answered quickly before getting out—hoping to avoid the argument that was brewing. Walking to the front of the car, I looked around, observing my surroundings before lifting the hood to mask my illegal smoking.

*Well*, it doesn't look that bad, but that's what they want you to think. Staring at the beautiful red brick building made me feel a little better, but I reminded myself not to get too comfortable. *They're not going to lock me up and have me hugging myself and bouncing off the wall,* I thought as I continued to smoke.

"Dre, you need to hurry up! Be done by the time I put our son in this stroller, and if not, you're throwing that away!" Tam scowled.

I took the last few hits and held them in, trying to savor the last of the Mohicans. After finally exhaling the smoke, I tossed the doobie down and stepped on it. I shut the car hood and sprayed myself to mask the weed smell. After letting my wife know I was ready, we made our way down the sidewalk toward the entrance. We walked through the main doors, got on the elevator, and went to the first door on the left as instructed. I couldn't believe what I saw. I was expecting crazy people fidgeting while hugging themselves, padded walls, and doctors forcing patients to take their psych meds from carts. Instead, it looked like an upscale, privately owned doctor's office.

"May I help you?" the sweet blonde-haired lady behind the intake desk asked. Suddenly, a door opened, and a tall, well-built black man came walking out, crying. Any little bit of comfort that I was feeling went out the window.

"Uh, I think we're lost. Sorry, we'll be leaving now," I lied, trying to get the hell out of dodge while I still had the chance.

"Excuse my husband, he's nervous. This is Andre Shephard," my wife butted in, while elbowing me. Just like always, as soon as I try to escape from my problems, my wife shows up and makes it impossible. Don't get me wrong, I do like the fact that Tam encourages me to fight instead of running away, but this was not the time.

"You must be his wife, Tamera, whom I spoke to on the phone. I'm Sarah, the administrative assistant."

"Yes, nice to meet you, Sarah," my wife acknowledged. Right on cue, Big Noodle, who must've felt left out, made his presence known with a loud baby coo.

"And who might this adorable little cutie pie be?" Sarah asked.

"This is my son Zion, but we call him Big Noodle," my wife answered.

After playing with Zion for a few seconds, Sarah reverted to her professional demeanor as she pushed the button to announce my presence.

"She'll be right with you," Sarah informed us.

"Who?" I asked.

"Oh, my apologies. I assumed your probation officer informed you of your required sessions with your case worker, Mrs. Karolyn." Sarah dropped the bomb.

I was so confused. To my knowledge, I was only here because I gave in to my begging wife. *What does she mean by " required,"* I thought. *See what I get for listening?*

Maybe 5 minutes passed before the door opened, and a black woman in her early 40s walked towards us and extended her hand. "Hello, I am Mrs. Karolyn. You must be Mr. Shephard," she said, introducing herself. "And you, my darling, must be his wife, Tamera, so I'm guessing this precious one is Zion," she smiled. Mrs. Karolyn was dressed as if she had just left church. Her style was giving off old school granny vibes; all she was missing was the big southern church hat.

I couldn't quite pinpoint it, but there was something about her presence that brought me peace. Of course, I tried to ignore it. I didn't speak; I just watched as she interacted with my wife. *Whatever this therapy is, I refuse to trust her. Especially since her assistant mentioned my probation officer. How the hell is he even involved?* I thought. *I know one thing, if she's talking to him, I ain't talking to her.*

"Well, Mrs. Shephard, I promise to return your husband to you safe and sound," she winked at Tam, smiling.

"Take all the time you need! Lord knows it could take his people 40 years to finally catch on," Tam joked with Mrs. Karolyn.

"Wait, you're not coming?" I was more nervous than I wanted to admit.

"Don't worry, Mr. Shephard, this is only the intake process," Mrs. Karolyn assured. "This is the easy part."

*I don't know if that was supposed to cheer me up, but epic fail,* I thought.

"Please follow me," she said, leading the way down the hall. Once we entered her office, a chill ran down my spine. There were crosses and scriptures all over the walls, like I'd imagine a pastor's office would look like.

*Aw, that explains the clothes. She's a Jesus freak,* I thought, taking it all in as I slowly reclined in the soft leather chair.

"Please make yourself comfortable, Mr. Shephard," Mrs. Karolyn said politely as she walked around the desk and settled in her chair. After viewing through a few files on her desk, Mrs. Karolyn looked up and asked, "Okay, Mr. Shephard, do you know why you're here?"

I remained silent, feeling set up. *She can keep me here all day, but I ain't saying shit!* I thought in frustration.

"So, Mr. Shephard, according to your probation officer and your wife, you have a smoking habit, care to explain?" she asked.

*What the hell? My wife told her I SMOKE? And why does she keep bringing up my probation officer?* I clenched my fist as my whole body tensed in rage.

The defensive look I gave her must have said it all. "Are you angry, Mr. Shephard?" she asked.

"Do you get paid to ask me these dumb ass questions, or is that what they taught you in college?" The words came out before I could even think. My attitude and level of no fucks given was at a ten.

She took her glasses off and set them on her desk. She folded her hands and took a deep breath in, and with the sweetest voice after being told off, she said, "Look, Mr. Shephard, I'm going to be honest with you, I'm here to help you. Now, before you roll your eyes, I do mean that. I know you probably heard this a million times, but I am being sincere. You have 11 dirty UA's, you haven't paid a dime for probation fees, you have a concerned wife who loves you, and you haven't even completed half of the required 10-year probation sentence. Do you want to go to prison? Because this is the last stop! After me IS prison," she spoke softly in a genuine tone that for some reason made me believe her. Still, I wouldn't give in.

She reached over and grabbed my hand. With a concerned look in her eye, and before I could pull back, her next words paralyzed me from the inside out. My heart stopped beating, my lungs stopped breathing, and my eyes started tearing up as her question echoed in my head. I fell into a deep daydream, **"Who is Zion Blake?"**

## 3. *The Run In*

*"Pride goeth before destruction, and an haughty spirit before a fall."*
**— Proverbs 16:18—**

"HHHHHEEEYYY GGGOOODD DAMN ME!" I yelled my signature greeting.

"HHHHHEEEYYY GGGOOODD DAMN ME!" the crowd shouted back right on cue, showing me love.

After making my grand entrance, I dapped all my homies up. One of the things I loved about Southwest High School was it felt like home, being that everyone pretty much grew up together. As I made my way through the hallway, my eyes were drawn to a pair of freshly manicured French-Tipped toes; a fetish of mine. I was in awe as my eyes caressed up her body until they locked in with the most gorgeous hazel eyes.

"Hey NiggaMan," she said, blushing.

NiggaMan was the nickname everyone called me. I introduced him during our Homecoming week in '05. The theme of the day was superheroes, and being the creative, comedic genius that I am, I came up with the greatest alter ego of all time, NiggaMan! I loved it because I thought it was clever, catchy, and most importantly, unique.

"What's good, ma?" I asked, giving her my best Lick Lip Cool J impression. I looked her up and down, rubbing my hands together like Birdman from Ca$h Money Records. "Don't move. You got something in your eye," I said smoothly, gaining her trust while baiting her in. "Hold on. Close your eyes. I'm going to blow it out for you," I continued, preying on her. I was so close at this point that I could feel her heart beating rapidly.

"Oh my God, what is it? Save me," she played along while closing her eyes.

"Don't worry, beautiful. I got you," I said, flattered. I placed one hand on her cheek and the other on the opposite side as I leaned forward to give her an unforgettable kiss. Her lips were soft and moist from the lip gloss she wore. Her eyes popped open in shock as a blush formed on her cheeks. She pulled back, but I could tell she liked it.

"Boy, you are not slick," was all she could mutter. Her body was telling her no, but her mind was telling her yes, or however that R. Kelly song goes that my mom listens to on her CD player. She flirtatiously hit me, which led to us playfighting. When the bell for first period rang, I wrapped my arm around her and escorted her to class. Once we approached, she turned toward me and gave me a tight hug, while secretly slipping a note into my backpack. "Thank you, NiggaMan," she said as she turned and strutted off in her Stiletto Pumps, Apple Bottom Jeans, and Baby Phat t-shirt that complemented her hourglass frame.

"No problem, ma. Holla at me after class, love," I shouted before turning to make my way to my first period. And that's why I'm that NiggaMan! I thought, feeling myself.

I had a big reputation to live up to because my older brother was popular. Wanting to outshine him, I saw each new day as an opportunity to keep everyone on their toes with my wardrobe selections. During the first week of school in August, I came wearing a tuxedo underneath a fake Chinchilla coat that hung down to my ankles. Everyone laughed and thought I was crazy for wearing fur in the Texas heat. The principal literally made me leave my coat in his office because it was distracting, according to him. Another day, I came dressed in my custom-made NiggaMan costume. I got suspended that day! Today's selection was another display of my style. I had on a purple-collared Ralph Lauren shirt that revealed my athletic frame, my icy-white Air Force 1s, and my "Starchy Archies," which the homie Little Brad used to call his starched pants.

My dark-skinned friends like to joke around by calling me the "Ultimate light skin." Little do they know that it only adds fuel to my fire. Someone has to be the one to bring us back into style.

You may think I have an inflated ego, but if you only knew me from 5th grade through middle school, you'd understand my confidence now. I was bullied by practically everyone for stress-induced bald spots in my hair.

One kid said, "It looks like Dre got an edge up with a can opener," and the whole class laughed, including the teacher. The teasing wasn't just at school, though. I also got it at home from Manny, my mother's boyfriend at the time. When I told her about his verbal abuse, she confronted him, but that only backfired.

He came to me and said, "Nigga, do you think I give a fuck you went crying to your mom? What the hell is she gonna do to me, Patches?" Clearly, he had no concern for my self-esteem, because from that day forward, until my hair grew back, "Patches" was the nickname he had for me.

During those hard times, I only had two real friends, Eric and Bob. It was hell growing up, but I quickly found that if I stood up for myself, others showed respect. Thankfully, my hair grew back just in time for high school. I went from getting "no play" to having all the girls flocking around me. Some swore I was Marques Houston's finer cousin, while others said I was Nick Cannon's light-skinned twin; either way, it boosted my confidence.

After finally making it to my classroom, I noticed we had a substitute teacher. Man, this sub doesn't know what he just got himself into, I thought, chuckling inside, knowing trouble was brewing.

"HHHHHEEEYYY GGGOOODD DAMN ME!" I yelled, making my entrance known.

"HHHHHEEEYYY GGGOOODD DAMN ME," the class responded, hyped up by my arrival.

"NiggaMan in da mutha fuckin building son!" I shouted with my East Coast accent. Everybody loved it when we had a substitute teacher, because that only meant one thing. I was about to act a damn fool.

"Alright, what an entrance. Now, if you will please find your seat and sit down, I can begin class," the fat old grumpy substitute demanded.

I went to my personally assigned seat, the very last chair in the back row. I sat down, reached into my backpack for a pen, and noticed a folded piece of paper. When I pulled it out, I saw it had my name on it. I undid the folding and began to read the letter.

*To: Niggaman*
*From: Devyn*
*Reason: I wanna be your Woman*
*Song: So confused*
*Lyrics: I wanna be your friend, your love, your all*
*Artist: Pretty Ricky*
*Request: That you be my Niggaman*
↓↓↓↓↓↓↓ *(drop down)*

*I know you don't know me, but I know you. I even braided your hair before, but I doubt you remember me since you got a groupie fan club now. Well, let me get to the point. I know you're a sophomore and I'm a fresh-wo-man, but I've been feeling you ever since I first saw you. I know you're single, but I wanna be Mrs. Nigga Woman. You might be thinking I don't even know you, but I know more than you think. I know you're about to be 16, March 5th, a Pisces, right? Your favorite color is blue, you obviously like football and basketball even though yo ass keep getting kicked off the teams. Am I right so far? Well, here's my number… use it: (817) 551-9642. If you call, I know you're feeling me.*

*Love Devyn*

*P.S. We should go to the movies…but don't think you're getting any! I ain't one of those fast ass girls in your little "fan club."*

I folded the note back into its original origami shape, wondering who had written it. Was it the same girl in the hallway, or someone else? I turned to my homie Spencer and asked, "Who is Devyn, bro?"

Spencer was my right-hand man. He was always down to join in my shenanigans, but out of respect for his mother, I never let him get into any real trouble because I knew the plans she had for his life.

"That's the freshman who braided your hair," he replied.

"What does she look like? Is she bad?" I asked, fixated solely on her appearance.

"Bro, you were just talking to her, doing that Rico Suave move in the hallway. I can't stand you light-skinned negros. El DeBarge-looking ass boy," Spencer joked. "Why do you ask, though? You trying to settle down and have a late-night special, Mr. Spectacular?"

I started reminiscing about her soft lips and how good she looked. "Me settling down, hell no. Why have one girl when you can have them all?" I spoke in the words of a true pimp. I handed Spencer the note so he could read it. By the time he finished, he looked up with a mischievous grin.

"Damn! Somebody stalking you, my boy, but shoot, what movie are we gonna go see?"

"Huh? What do you mean by " we? We ain't bout to go see nothin!" I replied, laughing at his sneaky way of trying to include himself.

"Bruh, she talkin' bout she not gonna give you none. We both know that's a lie," Spencer said, laughing.

"That's all y'all think about! My God, y'all can't talk about anything other than sex?" Jessica butted in after eavesdropping. Jessica was beautiful, with short honey-brown hair that complemented her caramel-colored skin. I once had a crush on her, but she's one of those control freaks with a lot of rules. Since rule number one was no sex for the first three months, she was instantly friend-zoned, which led to us becoming best friends.

"Girl, just because nobody wants your stuck-up ass doesn't mean we only want sex. Why are you always eavesdropping anyway? All in the Kool-Aid, but don't even know the flavor," Spencer clowned, causing the rest of the class to turn their attention towards us.

"Boy, don't nobody want y'all dusty UGLIASSES!" she fired back with full emphasis. It's as if she put "ugly" and "ass" together and made her own word.

"See? I wasn't going say anything to your bald-headed ass, but now I'm about to fire you up!" I joked with my best friend. At this point, I had the entire class's attention, as they knew it was showtime. *She got me messed up, calling me ugly, doesn't she know who I am? NiggaMan doesn't get clowned by anyone!*

"Who are you calling ugly? Over there looking like a snicker with elbows," I paused to let my audience get their laugh in. "Girl, you're so ugly Tom deleted you from his buddy list on Myspace! You over there looking like Chewbacca." The class erupted into laughter until the substitute had enough.

Attempting to cut the show short, the substitute teacher butted in, "That's enough!" Although he was trying to be serious, his voice cracked midsentence, which only made the class laugh even harder.

"Man, what was that? Tried to use your big boy voice, huh?" I said, making fun of him. "What do you mean by 'That's enough'? Do you know whose class this is? Yo, fat ass, better find out real quick, Sherman." Spencer was practically in tears as he caught onto The Nutty Professor punchline. The substitute teacher stood there glaring at me with hatred, but knowing that the show must go on, I added, "He is so fat, Jesus couldn't lift his spirits!"

"THAT'S IT! I will not tolerate you disrespecting me. Come get your write-up and make your way down to the principal's office, Mr. Comedian!" The substitute barked, embarrassed that he had been clowned by a 15-year-old.

*That's why he's a substitute and not a real teacher! He can't even control a classroom for an entire period, let alone a semester. Rookie!* I thought. I walked to the front of the class after gathering my things.

"Thank you," I said as I snatched the infraction from his hand. "Wait a second?" Holding in my laughter, I looked up from reading his name on the infraction. "You mean to tell me your name is really Mr. Sherman? Oh, Hercules, Hercules!! "Oh, my baby Sherman! Sherman, Sherman, Sherman," I continued with my Nutty Professor impersonation. At this point, Spencer dramatically fell on the floor laughing, while boo-jee Jess was unimpressed.

"GET OUT OF MY CLASSROOM!" the substitute yelled.

"Whew, sen-si-tive," I broke down the syllables like Major Payne as I walked out of the classroom. Pretending to be on my way to the principal's office, I made a quick pit stop at my locker to add the infraction to my growing collection. I grabbed my phone and texted Spencer to meet me in the bathroom after class, then headed in that direction. When I walked in, I immediately looked under all the stalls to see if anyone was in there. Exactly why I don't go poop at school. Not about to be identified by my shoes as the shitter, I joked to myself.

Suddenly, the door flew open, and an unfamiliar dark-skinned student rushed in. I had never seen him at my school before, and judging by the way he burst into the bathroom, I knew he wasn't supposed to be here. Who the hell is this athletic Akon lookalike, and why is he walking toward me? Lord, I hope I don't have to drop this nigga, I thought as the dark-skinned student approached.

"Yo, aren't you Jourdan's lil brother?" he asked as he extended his hand to shake mine.

I had never been happier to hear those words; usually, I hated being referred to as "Jourdan's little brother."

"Yeah, who are you?" I asked. Before he could answer, a loud knock banged on the bathroom door.

"Don't make me come in there! Come on out," Officer Terri's voice echoed off the bathroom walls. I knew it was Officer Terri because I've had many encounters with her.

The dark student panicked and ran into the stall, locking the door. A few seconds later, Officer Terri busted into the restroom. Pretending to be startled, I faked peeing. "Hey! Hey, this is the men's restroom! You trying to get a sneak peek at my goods?"

"Shut up, Mr. Shephard. I can clearly see you're faking. Besides, you don't have anything that'll impress me," Officer Terri shot back.

"Come on, what did I tell you about calling me by my slave name? My name is NiggaMan!" I corrected. That's when a loud burst of laughter came spewing from the stall where the unknown student ran.

"Yup, come on out, Mr. Banks. I knew you were in there," Officer Terri said, referring to the unknown student.

"Boy, you are funny as hell," he said, looking at me as he walked out of the stall.

"Now, Zion, you know I work at your school too. I don't even know why you would attempt this foolishness, knowing I'd recognize you. You're smarter than that and have a bright future ahead of you, as long as you stay out of trouble," Officer Terri said.

Zion? I pondered the name that sounded so familiar. Wait, Zion Banks? As in the fastest kid in Fort Worth, Zion? I suddenly remembered where I'd heard the name, but how does he know my brother? If I was correct, Zion was a student at North Crowley High School and a well-known track star. In his freshman year, he beat Landon, a senior who was being heavily recruited by some of the top D1 colleges.

"Why you gotta come ruin my fun, Officer Terri?" Zion asked, laughing as she ushered him out of the bathroom.

"You know it's against the rules to be on a different campus without permission, but lucky for you, I'm going to let this slide as long as you don't come back," Officer Terri told Zion. Not wanting to miss anything, I kept following them as the bell for the next period rang. The hallways began to fill with students, all eyes locked on us.

When we finally made it outside the school, Officer Terri released Zion's arm and told him to get off campus. He sprinted off like Usain Bolt, faster than anyone I've ever seen. When he took off, I saw a wallet fall out of his hoodie. Someone tried to pick it up, but I had to step in to get it. When I saw the wad of cash inside, I knew he'd be looking for it, so I decided to keep it safe until I could give it to my brother later.

"Do you know him, NiggaMan?" a female asked me from the crowd.

"Yeah, that's my cousin," I lied, once again putting the spotlight on me as I'd say anything to keep my popularity.

The rest of the day was uneventful; I couldn't wait to tell my brother about my run-in with Zion. As soon as I got home, I knocked on my brother's bedroom door and waited for permission to come in. When I entered, I saw Pat, Mallie G, and, to my surprise, Zion sitting on my brother's couch.

"Titties, anyone? **I said, titties, anyone?**" I smiled.

"TITTIES, BABY!!!!" Mallie-G responded to the little intro motto we created.

"What up, son?!" Mallie G said, shaking my hand.

"What up, B," I joked, mimicking his New York accent. "What up, Pat?" I acknowledged.

"What's up, NiggaMan?" Pat dapped me up.

"Yo, how do you know him, Jay?" I questioned my brother while we did our secret handshake.

"Who Zion? That's Pat's lil cousin," Jay replied.

"Oh ok. Wassup lil nigga?" I joked, as I was clearly shorter and much smaller than Zion.

"Little?" Zion laughed as he shook my hand.

"I was about to give this to my brother, but I guess since you're here, I can give it directly to you," I said, pulling out his wallet and handing it to him. His eyes lit up in excitement like it was Christmas morning.

"Bro, thank you!"

"No problem, fam," I replied. "You're lucky you knew my brother! Walking around with all that cash, you could've got jacked," I said, acknowledging I went through his wallet.

He counted his money, then took a crisp $20 bill out of the stack and handed it to me.

"Here, bro, thanks for being real," Zion said.

"Nah, thank you!" I was very excited because $20 only meant one thing: a dub sack.

"Bro, you are funny as hell. I can see why you're popular at school besides looking like an off-brand Nick Cannon," Zion cracked a joke to which everyone laughed.

At that moment, Jay's words replayed in my head again. He told me before I entered high school, "Wherever you go, make your name and presence known!" I've been striving to live up to that standard ever since.

## *4.Help Is On The Way:*

*"The Lord is nigh unto them that are of a broken heart; and saveth such as be of a contrite spirit."*
— **Psalm 34:18—**

"Mr. Shephard, what's going on in your head? You haven't said a word, yet you're visibly holding back tears. What is eating you up inside?" Mrs. Karolyn asked, snapping me back into reality. I sat in silence, mourning and refusing to let her in. Tears skied down my cheeks, sliding into the slippery slope of depression, or what you might call my heart. "Is that it? Is Zion the trigger for your sadness?"

I clenched at the mention of his name, and more tears began to flood. I can't take this anymore. Stop mentioning that name, please! I begged in my head, yet no words left my lips. As hard as I tried to remain, she was breaking me down, but I wouldn't budge.

"Ok, Mr. Shephard, it's clear to me you have a lot of pain and likely suffer from Major Depression because of your past traumas. I can't force you to say anything, but I see we have a long way to go! Due to time, we will pick this up where we left off tomorrow and—" she paused to let the suspense build. "I am scheduling you every day of this week, possibly the next, until I feel comfortable reducing our sessions from daily to three times a week." The words stopped the flow of tears and lit a flame of wrath within me.

"Are you kidding me? Every day of the week, for what?? You don't give a shit about me; you're just here to collect a check. All you want to do is punish me until I really do reach my damn breaking point." I said, aggravated. "So, what if I don't come? Hypothetically speaking."

"Look, Mr. Shephard, I know you don't like this, but according to your records, you have admitted to being suicidal in the past. Quite frankly, son, in my professional opinion, you really need help. You can't just bottle everything up until you explode. I mean,

I've been observing you throughout this session, and your body language says it all. You do realize that if you commit suicide, that is permanent! Let me help you before you reach that point," Mrs. Karolyn spoke with words of wisdom and empathy. "You should think about yourself, but if you can't do that, then at least think about your beautiful family. They need you! How would Zion feel, either one for that matter, if you committed suicide?" There was something about her words that made me feel semi-comfortable with her. She took her glasses off and looked deeply into my eyes as she grabbed my hand. "Listen, baby, you don't ever have to come back here if you don't want to, but then you would be refusing my help and basically telling the judge that you would rather spend your sentence in prison. Is that what you want?" she softly questioned.

"No, ma'am," I said, honestly afraid of going to prison. However, as soon as I broke my silence, my mind started questioning where she was getting the information from, because I rarely talk about that time in my life. In fact, only three people knew about my suicide attempts. I sat, confused, wondering whether to continue being mad or to pay close attention.

"Mr. Shephard, are you ok? Wait, do you like to be called that, or do you prefer to be called something else?" Mrs. Karolyn asked, making me more at ease.

"Dre. Call me Dre," I requested.

"You got it! Moving forward, I'll call you Dre," Mrs. Karolyn assured.

As we made our way back to the front, a feeling of guilt came over me, and I knew I owed Mrs. Karolyn an apology. No matter how I felt about being forced into therapy, she didn't deserve me snapping on her, but what could I possibly say to justify my behavior? When we reached the waiting room, I couldn't find my wife and son. I assumed they were in the car waiting for me, so I made my way down to the parking lot. After getting into the driver's seat, I told Tam everything that happened in the session, even how I snapped at Mrs. Karolyn.

"I didn't even apologize to her," I admitted, knowing my mother raised me better.

"Well, you can do it first thing tomorrow when you go back," my wife suggested.

I knew she was right, so I came up with a plan for the next session. I started the car and headed to pick up my oldest son, De'Andre. We called him Dre Dre because he was truly my mini-me and a third generation. I drove the 8 miles to Woodway Elementary School, which was the same school I attended as a child. When I pulled up, Dre Dre was playing with the other kids until he recognized my presence.

"Daddy!" he yelled, running towards me with a huge smile on his face.

""Wassup, lil man? How was school?" I asked.

"I got a green smiley face, daddy," he said, beaming with pride, as it indicated excellent behavior today.

"That's my boy! Now you're becoming a man."

"Yep, daddy, I'm a man," Dre Dre said, sticking out his chest like a superhero. I couldn't help but laugh, and his teacher, Ms. Anderson, who was approaching us, laughed along.

"So that's where he gets it from!" Mrs. Anderson said, answering her own speculation. "I told him earlier, 'boy, you're a trip,' after he made the whole class laugh. He responded that he wasn't no boy but rather a man like his dad. I thought that was so cute," Mrs. Anderson said, giggling.

"Boys like to be called men, so I praise him when he shows characteristics of becoming one. Like today, when he got a green smiley face," I said as I tickled my son to celebrate his good behavior once more. "But I also discipline him accordingly, like you witnessed a month ago," I refreshed her memory of me spanking my son for fighting in class.

"Oh yes, I remember!" Mrs. Anderson acknowledged with a smile. "He's been on his best behavior ever since, so thank you again. I wish there were more active fathers around here," she said, referring to the lack of present fathers in the African American community.

While I appreciated her acknowledgment, I hated the reality that so many kids grew up without male guidance. Man, I wish people would do better, I thought, until my son Patrick came to mind. I tried to remind myself that the situation was different to stop me from heading down a familiar road. Come on, you just got out of therapy. Can you not beat yourself up for at least one day? I asked myself, while doubting, if I could answer sincerely. I felt my son nudge me, which helped me come back to the present. Ever since that day, I could zone out at any moment, being trapped in my head, chained to my thoughts.

"Thank you," was all I said before walking Dre Dre to the car.

"Tam! Tam! Guess what?" Dre Dre screamed with joy from the back seat.

"What, pumpkin butt?"

"I got a green smiley face!" he squealed, satisfied with his performance.

"That makes three weeks in a row now. I think we should celebrate!" Tam cheered. "Look at you! You're becoming such a little man."

"Yep, I'm a man like my daddy," Dre Dre said in his best little-man voice.

"Stop at the store so we can get him a surprise," Tam demanded.

As I pulled up to the pump, I leaned back and gave my wife a look that let her know there was no way in hell I was going inside. Tam shook her head, but instead of arguing in front of the kids, she got out and went inside the store.

"Hey, Dad, can we go to Chuck E. Cheese?" Dre Dre asked his favorite question. "Since I've been a good boy," he added, buttering me up.

I laughed inside. Boy, he gets that manipulation side from his mama. "I don't know, son, we'll see," I gave my favorite answer to his favorite question.

"Okay," Dre Dre said in defeat, knowing that most likely meant no. "Hey, Dad?"

"Yes, son?" I responded—looking at him through the mirror.

"I wanna see Pat Pat," he confessed.

His words sucker-punched me in the gut—making me lose the strength to hold back my emotions. Patrick is my second child, whom I don't talk much about because of what his mother did three days after he was born. It's a touchy subject for me, partly because of my own relationship with my father, who was absent from my life. On three different occasions, my dad broke his promise to do better and stay out of jail so that we could finally meet. Unfortunately, of the two times in my life that I actually saw my father, both were when he was incarcerated. The first time I met him was through a glass window when I was 5 years old. The second encounter and the only time I ever physically embraced him was during a contact visit when I was 17 years old, after he had just been sentenced to life in prison. On that day, I made a promise to myself that I would be a better father to my kids than my father was to me. Part of that promise was that, no matter what difficulties I may be facing personally or with my children's mothers, I would keep them connected. I wanted them to be close, which is why it makes me sad that Patrick and De'Andre don't get the full benefit of growing up together, the way my brothers and I did. Don't get me wrong, Dre Dre does have Zion, but between the age difference and the fact that they are stepbrothers, who knows what their bond will grow into.

"Pray, son! Remember what I said about God?" I quizzed him, trying to capitalize on his short attention span.

"All things are possible," he shouted like a pastor in a child's body.

"That's right, son!" I said as my wife got back into the car.

"What's possible?" she asked, feeling left out.

"I was just telling our son that all things are possible with God," I explained.

"Oh yes, that's right, baby. ALL THINGS! Look at your dad, for example, he finally took his first steps toward receiving help," Tam joked, reminding me of my session.

Driving home, I thought about my earlier conversation with Mrs. Karolyn. Once again, I felt bad about everything. I could tell she was a good person, which only sparked my curiosity about her story. I mean, she was at least trying. Maybe she has a testimony, and maybe God is using her to help others. I recalled how some elders told me I had a calling on my life when I was a kid, but I certainly hadn't heard those words in a while. The idea that maybe the reason I've been going through so much was so God could use me, too, came to mind, but I quickly shot that down. I don't have the patience to talk to people. Besides, who would listen to me? Going from NiggaMan to Preacher Man, I'd be the laughingstock of Fort Worth. My enemies would definitely try me.

The rest of the night was peaceful and unusual because the nightmare didn't happen. I woke up the next day relieved and more confident that Mrs. Karolyn could really help me. I knew all I had to do was let my walls down, but first, there were a few things I had to get straight before I'd be willing to be completely open with her. Before bed, I thought hard about what I was going to say to her, but now I just wanted to speak from the heart. I knew the root of my message and remembered my mom's words: *"Son, it's not what you say, it's how you say it."*

I got dressed and made my way downstairs. Tam must have been in a good mood, because I smelled another delicious breakfast cooking.

"Good morning, my queen," I greeted her with a hug.

"Good morning, my king," she answered. "Ready for the big day?" Tam asked encouragingly.

"I am," I said anxiously. After breakfast, I left the apartment. Before heading to my appointment, I stopped to get Mrs. Karolyn a dozen roses to apologize for our initial session. Arriving early, I went through the same door as yesterday. Noticing that Miss Sarah was busy helping a client, I knew I had a small window of time to complete my mission. I passed by her desk, making it look like I was going to take a seat. When the coast was clear, I hurried and snuck to the back before the door could close. Hoping to surprise Mrs. Karolyn, I made my way to her office, but to my surprise, she wasn't there. Oh well, I thought. I'll just wait right here until she comes. About 20 minutes passed, and finally the door opened.

"Oh my God! Dre, you scared me half to death. What are you doing back here, and how did you get in?" Mrs. Karolyn asked as she caught her breath.

"I'm sorry to scare you, Mrs. Karolyn. I thought long and hard about our session yesterday," I began as she set her belongings down and got comfortable in her seat. "First, these are for you," I said, handing her the roses.

"Thank you, but what are these for?" she asked, confused.

"I want to apologize for yesterday. I know you were only trying to help me, but you have to understand. I have a hard time trusting people and letting my guard down. When I start feeling uncomfortable, my security walls go up, and I just close off," I admitted. "I want to start this process with you, but before I do, you have to promise me a few things," I demanded.

"Dre, I cannot—" she tried to speak, but I interrupted her.

"Look, Mrs. Karolyn, before you say you can't, just hear me out. Everyone I've ever loved or trusted has disappointed me in some way. So please, the first request is that you don't pass me off to one of your colleagues. I don't want to speak to anyone but you! The second request is that you don't give up on me, even if I'm being difficult, like I was yesterday. I know I can be stubborn, but I'm serious about getting help this time," I said as my eyes began to fill with tears. "Last, please don't judge me or talk down to me, because I do that enough in my head. So, if you can accept my apology and requests, then I'm ready to get started."

"Dre, I forgave you yesterday before you even left, but I definitely appreciate your apology," Mrs. Karolyn started.

"Secondly, I thought about our encounter all evening, and it dawned on me that you and I aren't much different. So, I'm going to do something I don't usually do because I believe that when God puts something on my heart, I must be obedient and follow His instructions. Four years ago, my sister had a baby, which was a special moment for both of us. Since I'm unable to bear children, being there when she gave birth was an indescribable blessing that my sister shared with me. I always wanted to see it. You know, the birth? I love children, and it hurts that I couldn't have one of my own, especially a son for my husband." Her voice got shaky as she reached for a Kleenex.

"After my sister left the hospital, I made it my duty to check in like a house nurse. I mean, I was the Godmother, so I had my rights," she joked a little to cheer herself up. "I would do anything to help my sister. She may have found it annoying at times, but this was the closest opportunity I could get to having a child of my own, so I wanted to take full advantage of supporting her," she shared. Ms. Karolyn's tears began to pour as the memory was clear as day in her mind.

"Well, after a few weeks of getting on my sister's nerves, she thought it would be a good idea if I just took my niece with me to my house. That way, my sister could get the full rest she needed while getting rid of me. Things were good, perfect even; I would go get my niece almost every other day. I had her so often that my sister literally had to make me give her back once; that's how attached I was to my niece. Well, one day I remember her crying, which woke me from my sleep. I rolled over and patted her back after giving her a bottle. I must have done all that semi-awake, because I forgot to flip her over onto her backside." Mrs. Karolyn said as she began to weep.

Seeing Mrs. Karolyn in pain broke my heart, because it reminded me of my mother growing up.

"Well, I woke up the next morning, and I looked over for my niece, but she was gone. I panicked as I felt something," she paused and took a deep breath before letting out a muffled cry mixed with words. "I felt something underneath me. It was the baby," she continued. "I had to tell my sister that I killed her only child by accident, because I was so tired that I didn't do what I knew to do."

Wow, I thought. I knew she had a testimony, but never could I have imagined this. I couldn't utter a word. I just sat there feeling bad for her.

"You know why I really can help you, Dre? Because I know exactly how you feel! Lonely, depressed, confused, hating the world, blaming yourself, all the what-ifs playing constantly in your mind," she said as if she read the emotions off my face. "I lost someone too, and she would've been four years old tomorrow. I understand your hurt, but I want you to know it's going to be ok, Dre."

Wow, there it is! The same old same as a rerun, I thought, pondering her words. Just when I started to like Mrs. Karolyn. It's going to be ok, Dre. I know how you feel, Dre. Let God handle it, Dre. Oh, and everyone's favorite, it's not your fault; this is part of God's plan, Dre! Well, I think God needs to come down here and share this miraculous plan, because I'm dying inside. I wept uncontrollably as a rush of guilt and anger overtook me, but then I caught myself.

"You know what? I'm so fucking tired of hearing that bullshit. *'It's going to be ok, Dre,'*" I mimicked. "Look, you have your story, but that's not my story! Nor is your pain! Don't try to compare your life to mine, because you don't know half of the hell I have been through. You can read all the files you want, but you'll never know me, the shit I lived through, or who I had to be to survive it as a Black man. We aren't the same!" I was hotter than fish grease.

"You're right, Dre. I don't know you beyond the files and the conversations I've had with people around you. I do know one thing, though, you're a child of God, as am I. Your mother raised you in the church, according to the phone conversation I had with her. I know our human minds cannot fully grasp all His righteous plans, but trust, He does have a plan. It's a perfect plan for you, just as He had for me. Just as He had for my niece and for Zion! Proverbs 3:5-6 Trust in the Lord with all your heart, Dre! Lean not on YOUR OWN understanding, Dre, but in ALL your ways acknowledge Him, and He'll direct your path," she recited. "James 1:2-3 says, Dre, count it ALL JOY when you fall into various trials and tribulations, knowing that the testing of your faith produces patience. You see, son, it's destined that we will all go through different trials and tribulations. Now, my story isn't your story, but both stories are worthy of God's Glory. I don't know about you, but when I first heard that scripture, saying to count it 'All Joy,' I had to question God myself. It didn't register until later in life what that truly meant: to count it all as joy. Here I am helping others who suffered from real-life events, and the way I see it, God needed me to experience something tragic so I could relate to my clients."

Hearing God's word thrown back at me calmed the storm inside. I felt the tension in my body ease up as she made it personal by adding my name. Scriptures were familiar to me because my mother would text me a different one every morning to encourage me. Despite my outburst, I was ready to give Ms. Karolyn another chance, but before I could get a word out, she continued.

"Listen, Dre, I don't know exactly how you feel. There will be a lot of things I surely will not understand, but I do know pain. So, if you want my help, I am here. If not, do not waste my time. I chose this job to help others in need, the way I was helped. People like me who experienced depression and might not have the proper tools themselves but are willing to go through the process to receive treatment." She walked to her purse and pulled out a cosmetic compact to conceal the evidence of her human side. It didn't take long for her to get back to her professional self, but before she fully converted, she walked toward me and grabbed my hands. "I will pray for you," Mrs. Karolyn said as she squeezed my hands.

Why does everybody say that, knowing they're not going to stop what they're doing to say a little prayer for me? I thought. Recognizing the look on my face, Mrs. Karolyn told me to bow my head and close my eyes. I was shocked, but I did as I was told.

"Dear Heavenly Father, we come to your throne humbled and thankful for your grace and mercy. Lord, without you, we'd be lost sinners. Lord, we thank you for sending Your only begotten Son to die for our sins, that we may be saved by His blood. We know that grace is showing love and kindness to someone because you chose to, and mercy is showing extra love to someone who doesn't deserve it. Lord, we do not deserve your grace and mercy, but we are truly thankful for them. I want to lift my client, my friend, my brother in Christ, Dre, to You, as he is lost and needs to be found. Lord, you said if two or more are gathered in your name, you will be there in the midst. You said if we knock, the door shall open. If we ask, we shall receive, and if we seek, we shall find. So, we are knocking on your holy door, asking you to come into Dre's heart and help him find you, especially when the devil attacks. Heal his brokenness and fill him with your love, because He who is in you is greater than he of this earth. Wrap Dre in your armor, Lord, shielding him from the wicked darts! I thank you for our trials and tribulations, which are too great for our human minds to comprehend. I pray that Zion is in heaven with you and that he knows he is truly missed and loved.

My eyes, now blurry from the overflow of sadness, opened at the mention of his name. Please, Lord, I thought in agreement. Then I wondered, how does someone thank God for their trials and tribulations? I felt chills flowing through my veins. I couldn't explain this feeling, but for the first time in a while, I felt at ease.

"Lord, I pray all of this in Your holy name," Mrs. Karolyn continued.

"Amen," we said in unison. Mrs. Karolyn hugged me and held her grip for a few seconds, even when I let go. I felt the love and concern through her tight squeeze, and I could no longer hold back my tears.

"I know it seems impossible, but don't look back! Focus on right now. A baby step a day is all it takes," Mrs. Karolyn said after releasing me from her embrace. At this point, I didn't know what to think. It was a lot to take in, but I just nodded to let her know I was listening. "So, since you're early and willing to open up, let's take advantage of the extra time we have and get to work," she said, taking a seat in her chair.

"I don't know what to say or where to start," I confessed.

"Not a problem at all. First, let's start small and work our way up. I'll just ask you some questions based on the files I received," she said, looking over her notes. "I see you have a smoking problem. When was the first time you smoked?" me from snitching, he told me if I didn't hit the blunt, he would hit me, '*Hit this cuz, before I hit you.*'" I mimicked.

"That's child abuse! Is he still around?"

"No ma'am. He and my mom split after he put a gun to her head and took my little sister," I said. "He snuck in through the window while my mom was asleep. When she opened her eyes, there was a barrel in her face and he demanded his daughter. To this day, I still don't know how we made it out of that situation, but that was only the beginning of what was to come," I ended.

Mrs. Karolyn sat there with a puzzled look on her face. "Did he go to jail?" she asked, curious for more information.

"My mom called the police, but these cops don't care about us Black people!" Hearing myself, forced me to reflect on my many encounters with police, as well as the media stories showing innocent unarmed African Americans killed in this country.

"What is your issue with the police?" Mrs. Karolyn asked.

"I'd rather pass on that question," I said abruptly.

"Aw, I see," she said, noticing how I switched up. "Okay, well, tell me about your childhood," Mrs. Karolyn asked, changing topics.

"There's really not much to tell. I hated my life as a child because I had bald spots and everyone made fun of me, including my mother's ex-husband." The thought of him made my body cringe. "I only had two true friends who never cracked a joke at me, and that was Eric and Bob," I laughed, thinking of my childhood best friends.

"What's funny?" Mrs. Karolyn asked.

"I told you how my mom had 6 kids, but I didn't tell you how I used to give her the most hell growing up. She tried her best, but after watching Boyz in the Hood, I think she felt like Mr. E could take on Laurence Fishburne's role and give me the male guidance I needed. Since Mr. E was a single father, she trusted him and allowed him to take me to football practice with Eric and to come talk to me when I got in trouble at home. Well, one day my mom gave him full permission to whoop my ass.

That day, Eric and I just happened to get off at the wrong bus stop while trying to mack with some honeys. His dad pulled up so quickly that he embarrassed us. He made us get into the car, and when we got to his house, he ordered Eric to go get the belt. I paused, chuckling at the thought of how scared Eric looked. Now I'm not going to lie, I was thinking Eric was about to get torn up, and I was ready to laugh from my front-row seat. When Eric came back with that thick-ass belt, I thought he was the dumbest kid alive. Personally, I would've gotten the thinnest belt I could find," I chuckled. "Anyways, Mr. E. put on Juvenile and turned the music up loud. Eric's face was priceless; he looked like a cow heading to be slaughtered. WAP! WAP! WAP! Man, he was whooping Eric's tail—having him scramble all over the ground, as I sat there trying hard to hold my laughter in. When he finished, I thought he was about to take me home, but he had other plans. Mrs. Karolyn, when I tell you I got my ass whooped like never before, I mean it! Years later, he was a teacher at my high school for the bad students, and when he would come talk to me, all I could remember was that ass-whooping," I ended.

"Oh, I like Mr. E. Sounds like you could have used a few more men like him in your life," Mrs. Karolyn teased.

Yeah, if I had a father like Eric's, I wonder where my life would be, I thought. "You're right, but shortly after that, we moved. Sadly, I never saw Eric or his dad again," I said, feeling the empty hole where my childhood friend left. "That was the first person I cared about who left my life," I added.

"I'm sorry, Dre. Sounds like both Eric and his dad made an impact on you as a kid. Let's jump ahead. Tell me about your kids. Start with Patrick," Mrs. Karolyn changed the topic again. How does she know about Patrick? I thought, as my emotions flared

. "Patrick is my second child. His mother and I fell in love briefly during high school, but Patrick's grandmother didn't approve because I was 17 and her daughter was 15. Well, I used to go over there a lot, especially when she got pregnant, which only made her mother call the cops on me when I refused to leave. On the day of his birth, she didn't even let me get in the car to ride with them. So instead, I rode my bike 20 miles to the hospital to see my second son being born. When they were released from the hospital three days later, I had my mother drive me to her house with a box of diapers and wipes. I knocked on the door, but no one answered. I knocked louder and louder, until finally a neighbor came out and told me they left early to move back to Louisiana. My heart was so crushed. I still don't understand why they would take my child away from me without even giving me a chance to be a father." At this point, I was overwhelmed thinking of Patrick.

"I'm sorry that happened to you, Dre," she said, pausing at the sight of my hurt. "You were so young," Mrs. Karolyn chimed in. We sat silently for a moment before she said, "Let's step away from Patrick for a little while and let's talk about your oldest, De'Andre. I'm assuming Patrick and De'Andre have different mothers. What's your relationship like with his mother?" Mrs. Karolyn questioned.

"Yes," I took a deep sigh, not knowing where to begin. "De'Andre's mother was my first, but she was also…" I paused. "She's also my stepfather's sister," I told the secret I liked to keep to myself.

"Wait? Wait! So, De'Andre is technically your son and step-cousin?" She asked the same question as everyone else when they first heard the story. I hated addressing it! De'Andre is my son, and there is nothing in this world that could ever make me ashamed or turn my back on him.

"Technically, yes, but let me explain—" I began.

## *5. Crossroads:*

*"Even though I walk through the valley of the shadow of death, I will fear no evil:
for thou art with me; thy rod and thy staff they comfort me."*
— **Psalm 23:4**

"Hey son, I want to talk to you," my mother said in an unusually soft-spoken tone that sent chills down my spine. I couldn't quite figure it out, but judging by her tone, I knew it had to be serious.

"Wassup, T-lady?" I replied, using the nickname people from Fort Worth used for their mothers. She gave me the What did I tell you about calling me that, look.

"Well, as you know, Manny and I have been dating for a while now," she stated.

A little too long, if you ask me. I kept that thought to myself. I hated Manny. I know hate is a strong word, but out of all the men my mom dated, I feared him the most. Besides being an O.G. Crip from one of the most dangerous hoods in Fort Worth, he had a history of going back and forth to prison, and let's not forget his track record with women. Rumor had it he badly beat one ex and even put a shotgun in her mouth, so why would I want a man like that dating my mother and repeating history? At this point, he had never laid a hand on my mother or us, but I knew it was only a matter of time. When he got mad or paranoid, there was another side of him that was aggressive, and the emotional abuse he inflicted made me fear what was to come.

"So, we've decided—"

"NO!" I interrupted before she could finish. I don't care what comes next, but if he is part of her "we," then it's a hell no for me, I thought.

"You didn't even let me finish. I was going to say we've decided to get MARRIED!" She said with excitement.

"WHAT!?" I yelled in shock. "Mom, NO! Why would you marry him?" I asked.

"Because I love him! Son, when you're older, you'll understand," she answered.

I wasn't okay with this at all. In fact, Manny's sister Teela came to mind. Although Manny was the oldest of their mother's twelve children, Teela was the third youngest and my age. Ever since we met the family years ago, she and I have liked each other from the start. We went from holding hands to "hunching" in the living room. Hunching was a word kids in the South used because we had no clue what we were doing when it came to sexual activity. Of course, when we got older, we figured it out. Teela was my first love; everyone knew we were a thing long before Manny and my mother got acquainted.

"Mom, what about Teela?" I made another attempt to derail this wedding train.

"Son, what y'all have is just puppy love. You're too young to know what love is," my mother informed. "We are the adults; y'all are the children. So, y'all need to cut that off because we are getting married."

I thought of everything I could say to change her mind. "Ok, mom, choose!" the spirit of rejection in me demanded. First it was your boyfriends, and now Manny. I thought as I once again felt abandoned by my mother.

"Choose what?" My mother asked with a confused look on her face.

"Choose between Manny and me," I begged—hoping this time I'd be her first choice. "You choose everyone else over me. When do I ever come first?"

Tears began to fill my mother's eyes as she was conflicted between choosing the love of her life or her teenage son. "Dre, you may not agree with my decisions, but one thing I will never do is put anyone above you. You are my son, my flesh and blood. I love

You, infinity! But this is a different kind of love. I am doing this because he makes me happy.

I know that's what she deserves, but I also knew Manny couldn't keep up this façade forever. Feeling vulnerable, I left the house. I decided to change my mood by meeting up with my best friend. Ever since I returned his wallet, Zion and I have built an unbreakable bond and have been rocking together ever since. Once we got close, Pat, Mallie G, and Jay rarely wanted to hang out with us; they saw us as annoying little brothers who were always pressing buttons. During times like this, Zion was the only person I could truly confide in.

"Got blunt?" Zion asked, mimicking the movie How High.

"Got weed?" I responded, as Redman. That was our thing; we linked up daily, smoked, hollered at chicks, or got into some kind of trouble.

"I see you got on your walking forces," Zion clowned—laughing as he looked down at my beat-up Air Force ones. He had a very distinct and annoying laugh. Imagine the hyenas on The Lion King, but only louder and more obnoxious.

"Boy, I know your Akon-looking ass isn't trying to high-side. You so black when you spit it looks like soy sauce," I fired back. High-Siding was something we did every day—making fun of each other or any random person nearby. Nothing personal; we just made humor out of everything. "But in all seriousness, I have to tell you something," I informed Zion as I changed the topic.

"Wassup? Bro, you know you can tell me anything," Zion assured.

"Man, would you believe my mom and Manny are getting married?" I spilled the bad news. "I told her to choose between him and me, but in the politest way, she chose both of us. Now, if Jourdan made her choose, I wonder what her answer would have been," I said, filled with envy. Besides my mother, every man she dated favored my older brother and punished me. They would give him special privileges that I wasn't allowed, even though he was only two years older than me. Zion was about the same age as his cousin, so he understood my frustration, which was another reason we were so tight.

"Damn, mama needs love too, Jody," Zion joked. He always knew what to say, and this Baby Boy line was perfect. "Just kidding, bro. I get it, but if mama is happy, then all we can do is support her. BUT—" he emphasized. "Stay on guard, just in case we have to fuck him up," he finished, giving me more assurance. Just hearing Zion have my mom's back meant the world to me. Since we were together almost every day, he grew to love and respect her so much that he started calling her "mama."

"I guess you're right, but if he lays one hand on her, I'm definitely going to fuck him up," I promised.

"WE! We are going to fuck him up," he once again included himself. I was grateful he was there to help calm me down. After finishing the blunt, I made my way back home.


Just 14 days after the bombshell wedding announcement, my mother and Manny were married in an African-themed ceremony to honor her Nigerian roots.

This wedding is bullshit, I thought. Look at him pretending to be a sweet, swole teddy bear in front of my grandma and grandpa. If they only knew.

When the pastor asked if anyone objected to the union, it took every bit of strength I had to remain silent. I've embarrassed my mother plenty of times, but I knew better than to do it on her wedding day. Besides, I've never seen my mother so happy. She looked like a beautiful angel walking down that aisle, like all her dreams were coming true. She had a bridal glow that only women who've been married could understand. Sadly, that was the last genuine smile I would see on my mother's face for a while.

After the wedding, we all moved into a two-story house. Once we finally settled in, the newlyweds decided to go on a date— leaving us kids home alone.

"Aye, Jay?" I yelled at my older brother. Every time my mother left us alone, I took it upon myself to annoy him.

"What?" Jay replied, anticipating my antics.

"Guess what?" I asked, snickering.

"What Dre?"

"Chicken Butt!" I couldn't help but burst into laughter— loving the irritated look on his face.

"Leave me alone and get out of my room," Jay demanded.

"I'm not in your room. Technically, I'm in front of your room," I corrected.

"Ugh!" Jay groaned. He tried to slam his bedroom door, but I put my foot in the way before it could fully close.

"Aht aht ahh, not so fast, young grasshopper," I taunted, pissing him off even more.

Suddenly, the door flew open and slammed against the wall. "Get the fuck away from my room!" Jay shouted, irritated by my childish behavior. He then looked at the wall behind the door. "Now look what you did."

I checked and saw a hole in the wall caused by the doorknob. "What the hell? Nigga, that was your dumb ass, opening the door all fast like your bout to do something." At this point, I was intentionally provoking him, knowing that my older brother wouldn't actually fight me.

"Yeah, whatever! I'm telling mom you did it. You know she ain't about to believe shit you say," Jay replied. He was right; my mother didn't believe a word I said half the time. In my defense, I only lied to get out of trouble, which was often.

"You right, so do what you gotta do. I'm used to getting punished for the crimes y'all committed," I said as I left to enjoy the last bit of my freedom. If I were going to be grounded anyway,

I might as well have some fun first. I walked to the Candle Tree Apartments, which was the go-to spot in the summer. I could hear a lot splashing from a distance, so I knew it was jumping.

"HHHHHEEEYYY GGGOOODD DAMN ME!" I yelled, announcing my presence.

"HHHHHEEEYYY GGGOOODD DAMN ME," everyone in the pool area screamed back.

As I got closer, I noticed the keys to the office golf cart were still in the ignition. *Perfect! Wait till they see this,* I thought. I hopped in the golf cart, slammed it in reverse, and floored it. Everybody ran out of the pool area to get a better view.

"Hey, get off that!!" the maintenance man yelled as he ran towards me.

"Go NiggaMan! Go!" the crowd cheered as if I was about to score a touchdown. I went as fast as the golf cart would let me, swinging left to right so he wouldn't get me.

"NiggaMan is a fool," I heard Jessica yell as everyone else laughed.

With the maintenance man still chasing me, I turned the corner to get some distance between us. Immediately, a truck cut me off, and the driver got out. *Oh shit! He's got to be one of them,* I thought as I literally hopped out while the cart was still going. The driver's face turned red when it crashed into his truck.

"What the hell?" the truck owner furiously screamed as he looked at the damage. "Get his ass," he barked to the other crew member.

"Run NiggaMan!" the homies yelled.

Feeling them on my heels, I took off running like I was being chased by a dog. I quickly made a sharp left and squeezed between the bars that gated the apartment complex. I was safe, but I just kept running like Forrest Gump. Clearly, I must have forgotten about the incident with Jay, because I ran home right into some trouble.

"Why the hell did you put a hole in the wall?" my mother scorned.

"I didn't! That was Jourdan," I corrected.

"Why are you lying?" Jay blurted out as he was clearly eavesdropping from his room. "You pushed the door open after I tried to shut it."

"Nig—" was all I could get out before my mother's right hand connected to my cheek. The slap came too fast to block or dodge. "Ouch!" I squealed.

"First, what did I tell you about saying that word? Secondly, I don't want to hear it. It's sad, Dre, you lie so much I don't know when you're telling the truth." My mother finished.

My jaw clenched, and my fists tightly squeezed as my anger was at an all-time high. *Oh hell nah! She got me messed up,* I disrespectfully thought. *Why the hell does she believe him all the damn time? Especially when I'm finally telling the truth.* All the suppressed emotions were raging in my head. *She didn't even choose me! She always favors Jay. Letting him stay out all night, but I gotta be in when the streetlights come on. Oh, and Manny? He's been getting a lot more comfortable lately, yelling at me like he's my daddy. Bet! All y'all got me messed up,* I concluded my final thought.

"That's what I'm talking about! You always believe anything he says and never give me the benefit of the doubt to even explain. Jourdan said it, so it must be true! You act like Jourdan never told a lie before. Y'all always favor him and let him do whatever he wants, but I must obey all these stupid rules. What is it, mom? You don't love me?" I said, feeling emptiness from the lack of attention. This time, I didn't care how it came across; I was beyond hurt. "You always choose Jourdan over me mom. Then Manny, who's next?" All the pain I secretly held in started to boil over.

Next thing I knew, Manny burst through the front door and slammed it shut. *Did he hear me? Oh well, if he did so what?* I thought. *What is he going to do? Whoop me? I wish he would. He ain't my daddy!*

"WHO THE FUCK ARE YOU TALKING TO?" he growled. I sat on the couch and ignored his question. "Oh, so I'm talking to myself?" Manny asked rhetorically.

I kept ignoring him and started flicking through channels until I stopped on Dave Chappelle. I began to fake laugh at the rerun episode I'd seen a million times.

"This is the bullshit I'm talking about. He may disrespect you, but he got me fucked up!" Manny hollered at my mother. Furiously looking at me, he turned the TV off and stood in front of it. "So, you find yourself ignoring me, huh?"

Oh, wow, you turned the TV off. Big deal! I got the remote, stupid. I picked up the remote control and tried to turn the TV back on. In the blink of an eye, he was standing over me and snatched the remote out of my hand. I got up to walk to my room, but he pushed me down and demanded that I remain seated.

"Get up again and see what happens," he threatened.

My curiosity overpowered my fear as I got up to see what exactly would happen. Keeping his promise, Manny picked me up and slammed me down on the ground. It was so fast I couldn't counter. I tried to push him off me and break free from his grip.

"Get the fuck off me!" I screamed. I used all the strength I had to fight back, but it wasn't enough.

Manny balled up his fist and held me down with his forearm. "Move again and I'll break yo mother fuckin jaw."

I stared into his eyes in disbelief, but they told me not to test him this time. My vision blurred from my tears as I looked over to my mother for help, but she stood there speechless, frozen from shock.

"You're not my daddy, get off me," I pleaded in defeat. When Manny finally released me, I was shaking from the adrenaline and hurt. Why didn't anyone help me? They both just stood there, letting him manhandle me like a fucking rag doll and not say a damn word! My pride and heart were crushed.

"I don't give a fuck, but you will not disrespect her or me. You only get one mother in life, so I bet not ever catch you disrespecting my wife again or I'll break your fucking jaw. You hear me?" He clarified. When I didn't respond, that only made him madder. He cocked his arm back and threatened to punch me, "I said do you hear me?"

"Yes," I finally gave in before I was dismissed.

I walked upstairs to my room and laid silently on my bed. I stared at the ceiling as the recent memories started replaying in my mind. No longer could I stop the pain from pouring out. I knew we would see this side of him, but I never expected it so soon after the wedding. My mind recalled the incident from the past week. I saw my mother crying and him mumbling under his breath for her to go upstairs. I didn't know what was going on, but I knew it was my duty to protect my mom.

Following his orders, she started walking up the stairs, but stopped midway and said, "You know what, just do it right here. Why go upstairs? Just do it in front of my kids." I didn't know what she meant, but it pissed Manny off.

"Play with me if you want to," I remembered he said, nonchalantly but with a threatening tone, as they continued walking. When they closed their bedroom door, I tiptoed up the stairs and went to my sister's room, which was next to their room. I gently placed my ear on the wall so I wouldn't be caught eavesdropping. I could no longer hear my mother's cries, indicating he had taken her into their walk-in closet to muffle the sound. I wanted to kick the door down to save her and was about to until I heard him say, "Bitch keep fucking playing with me, and I'll kill you and your kids."

I felt myself getting triggered all over again by the memory. *I hate him! I knew he was like this, but I can't believe my mom just let him do that to me!* Then a soft knock on my door snapped me out of my thoughts. I wiped away the tears and bottled up my feelings to release them later.

"Hey son, are you ok?" My mother's soothing tone untwisted the lid off my emotional bottle.

"Mom, why didn't you help me? Or at least stop him?" I could no longer contain my emotions. Although the feeling of betrayal overwhelmed me, I couldn't help but notice the state of my mother, whose eyes were now overflowing with tears of her own. It was as if she saw the condition of my heart through her maternal lens.

"Son, I'm going to be honest," she began, as her heart took on the burden of mine. My mother began to cry loudly, sobbing as she lifted her sleeve. I knew Manny must have left because he didn't tolerate my mother crying, nor did he tolerate us kids, for that matter.

When I looked down at my mother's arm, I noticed a fresh bruise. I felt a homicidal urge, but my mother grabbed my arm, stopping me from getting up.

"No, baby, please sit down and listen. I don't have much time before he comes back," my mother begged. As rebellious as I usually am, for some reason, I obeyed. "I confronted Manny for what he did to you, but that only backfired. Maybe I caused this by talking back, but I just wanted to show you because—" she paused as the last string holding her heart together snapped. She hugged me tightly and cried into my arms. "I want to apologize for not protecting you, but I was afraid. He is beginning to get worse, so let's pray for him."

My mother's words felt like another slap to my face. I didn't want to pray for him. I wanted her to leave him, but my mother is a woman of God. Regardless of how hard times got, prayer was her answer for everything.

"Bow your head and close your eyes. Pray with me, son," my mother begged.

I bowed my head, but I didn't close my eyes. I sat there thinking. I knew this day was coming. Just wait till I tell Zion.

"Dear Heavenly Father, we come to your throne, humbled and thankful for your mercy. We ask that You forgive us for our daily sins from the past, present, and future. Lord, we lift Manny up to you and pray that You give him a clean heart. We ask that You uproot the roots of evil that have been embedded in him. Clear his mind and steer his anger away. Lord, I also ask that You protect me and my children. Protect us with Your armor. In Jesus' name, we pray. Amen," she closed.

# *6. Calamity Calls:*

*"Many are the afflictions of the righteous, but the Lord delivers him out of them all."*
**—Psalm 34:19 (NKJK)—**

I wish I could tell you my childhood got better, but it didn't. In fact, things got even worse. Months flew by, and it felt like we were living with the Devil. Manny had become more of an alcoholic—making it hard to mask his internal demons. On my 15th birthday, he was so drunk that he forced me to drink his Big Gulp cup filled with E&J and Coke until I finished it. He said if I threw up, he would punch me in the chest for wasting his liquor. That was just one instance of his abuse, but of course there were dozens more. No longer were my mother and I praying for Manny to change; instead, we were asking God to help us safely escape. However, that felt like an impossible task, given that my mother worked full time, had six kids, and a husband who never left the couch.

Daily, my mother begged me not to do anything stupid. Not only did she fear Manny, but also the retaliation of his other 10 siblings. I said 10 because Teela was neutral. She knew what her brother was doing to us was wrong, but she had enough sense not to go against him. However, the other siblings were loyal to him, which meant they couldn't be trusted. Sadly, I learned that the hard way. I slipped up and told Manny's little brother, who was close to Jay's age, that if he hit my mother again, I was going to whoop his ass with a bat and then call the police. Of course, he went back and told Manny. I was in the kitchen washing dishes, as usual, when my mother got the call.

"Andre, what did you do?" My mother's eyes were full of fear.

"I don't know," I replied cluelessly.

"Look, baby, I can't save you when you lie to me. I need you to always tell me the truth so I can try to protect you. Manny is on his way home, pissed off because he was told you were going to call the cops on him. You know how he feels about cops! Now I'm supposed to take your phone and make you wait here until he gets home. Baby, what did you do?" Her tone let me know she was afraid, so I told her everything I said to Manny's brother.

"Why would you do that? That didn't make any sense, and now you've put everyone at risk. You know how he gets when he's drunk and paranoid," my mother said fearfully. "Never mind that. Let's pray."

After we prayed, I heard the loud bass of Manny's speakers blasting as he pulled into the driveway. I was so afraid, I couldn't move. The flashback from Thursday came to mind when I had to use myself as a human shield to stop the blows from landing on my mother's body. The bass made me wince, and I could still feel the pain in my ribs.

Boom! The door was kicked open. "Where the fuck is he?" Manny hollered as he searched for me. As my mother and I locked eyes, everything began to feel like it was moving in slow motion. My heart dropped when her eyes widened at the smell of E&J. Suddenly, Manny snatched me by my ponytail, threw me on the floor, and started stomping on me like I was one of his worst enemies.

"AAAWWW MMMMAAAMMMAAA!!" I cried. "I'm sorry! I'm sorry. Please stop," I begged as another powerful blow to my stomach landed from Manny's kicks. "I can't …breathe," I gasped.

"Baby, please stop," I heard my mother beg.

"You want yo ass beat next, bitch?" Manny yelled as he turned in her direction. Fearing he would finish taking his anger out on my mother, I did what I knew not to do.

"I swear I'm calling the police on your ass! I HATE YOU," I uttered the words I soon regretted saying.

Like an angry bull, Manny took his attention off my mother and came charging to finish me off. He punched me, kicked me; he did everything he could to release his anger. I didn't know if I I would survive this attack because he showed no restraint with my teenage body. Finally, my brother came home and grabbed Manny off me. I looked down at my bruised limbs from a fetal position to a sight that still hurts me to this day.

"Calm down, that's my little brother! You can't be stomping on him like he's one of these niggas in the streets," Jay defended.

"You right, you right. I'm sorry, Dre. I shouldn't have let my anger get the best of me. Let's go smoke, Jay," was all I got for the brutal attack I just endured.

Right, let's stop whooping my ass because Jay's here, I thought. For some reason, Manny never showed his true colors when Jay was around, but since Jay was often gone, that gave Manny a big window to do shit. After Jay and Manny went to smoke in the garage, Teela and my mother rushed to my aid. Ever since the wedding, Teela had been at our house every other day and had witnessed a lot of her brother's antics. This time was unlike the others, and she knew he had gone too far.

When the garage door opened, everyone jumped back into their original routine as if nothing had happened. I quickly wiped away my tears, knowing Manny didn't approve of boys crying. He looked at me for a few seconds, then turned to my mother. "Let's go get something to eat."

After they left, Teela grabbed my hand and led me to my room. I knew where this was going because we always seized the opportunity whenever Manny and my mother weren't home. When we got to my room, she threw me on the bed and said, "I know what'll make you feel better... something your girlfriend Stray could never do." Teela was cocky, which I liked about her. She knew my girlfriend's name but refused to acknowledge it. Even though Teela and I were off and on, she felt very possessive of me since we were each other's first.

Still sore from Manny's vicious attack, I decided to accept Teela's offer to make me feel better. Midway through her topping me off, the beating started replaying in my head. Trying to shake off the distraction, I instantly picked her up and started doing what I saw Mr. Marcus do on Manny's sex tapes. When I heard Manny's bass approaching, I stroked harder to take out my frustration. A few seconds later, we both collapsed, breathing heavy as we climaxed at the same time. When the bass turned off, I quickly jumped up and ran to the shower, while Teela got herself together. We almost got caught a few times, but this time was so close I forgot to pull out.

After I got dressed, I asked my mother privately if I could go see my girlfriend Tay to get some fresh air. I didn't want to ask her in front of Manny, because I knew he'd say no for her. Once she said yes, I quickly left to avoid any interaction.

Tay often stayed at her sister's apartment, which was just a few blocks away. Since her sister was hardly ever home, it was easier for us to be alone. I really loved and cared for Tay. She was light-skinned, very beautiful, and although she was only fourteen, her body was well-developed and curvaceous.

"Dre, we need to talk," Tay informed me as I sat on the couch.

"Wassup, love?" I never liked how these conversations went.

"Dre, I'm pregnant," Tay admitted. I looked at her and then at her stomach in shock. A jolt of excitement ran through my body. I might have only been fifteen, but I was ready to be a father. Or so I thought.

As excited as I was, the next thought I had was Manny finding out and the beating I'd receive, so we decided to keep the news to ourselves.      About a week passed after Tay told me the news, and I had just linked up with Zion.  I decided to inform him about everything that was going on, including Tay and I plans to run away.

"My boy is about to be a daddy?" Zion questioned. "Are you ready?"

"Hell no," I laughed. "But what choice do I have?" Suddenly, my phone rang. Ugh, what the hell does Teela's sister want? I thought. I didn't like Teela's younger sister; she was beyond annoying.

"Hello," I answered.

"Dre, I have to tell you something because Teela is too scared," she began.

"Scared to tell me what?" I asked as my stomach knotted up.

"Teela is pregnant."

My heart stopped, and my lungs stopped breathing. Oh boy, I am in some shit now. I hung up the phone. Immediately, a million thoughts ran through my mind. Damn, what is Manny going to do when he finds this out? How did this happen? Shit! What about Tay? I knew I needed to update Zion on the phone call.

"Wait, wait!" Zion said between laughs. "So, Manny is fucking your mom, and you pay him back by getting his sister pregnant?" It was so funny to him, but to me it was the scariest feeling ever. "So, the baby is going to be your child slash stepcousin?" Zion was on a roll. "This is some Jerry Springer shit for real!"

I immediately ran home and began packing a bag to run away. Luckily, Manny wasn't there, so I tried to hurry. Before I knew it, the door opened, and it was him. I walked downstairs with my bag and tried to leave, but he stopped me.

"What's up, son?" Manny asked, knowing I hated it when he called me that.

"Nothing. I was gonna go to Will's house and spend the night, if that's cool," I said, trying to walk and talk.

"Before you go, wash the dishes," he ordered. I was so relieved. Clearly, he still hadn't received the news. Not caring that it was Jay's dish day, I quickly went to the kitchen to complete the task.

Then I heard his phone ring. Something about his ringtone sent goosebumps down my spine; I just knew it was the call I'd been dreading.

"WHAT?" I heard Manny yell. "ANDRE, bring your ass here! Jourdan, go get my strap!"

I bolted—fearing for my life. By the time I got through the first lock on the front door, Manny yanked me back and threw me onto the living room floor.

"What's wrong? What happened?" Jay asked as he and my mother ran to my rescue, or so I thought.

"This dumb-ass motherfucker got Teela pregnant!" Manny roared. My mother's eyes were at first saddened, then she quickly frowned in anger. She walked over to me and started hitting me. Happy with the woman he created, Manny stepped back to let my mother get some licks in.

"Jourdan, hurry up and go get my strap!" Manny ordered again, but Jay just stood there with tears in his eyes.

"I can't do that, Manny. I know you're mad right now, but he's still my little brother. You can't shoot him; I won't let you." All the love I had for my brother deepened after that moment. "If you're mad at me, I get it, but you'd have to shoot both of us," Jay stated firmly.

By the grace of God, I survived that day, but Manny never let it go. He ordered Teela to get an abortion, but she refused, which only made him more furious. To make matters worse, once their mother found out, she snapped at Manny and told him it was his fault for letting it happen under his roof. For weeks, I walked on eggshells, fearing that Manny would shoot me in my sleep. Just when I thought things couldn't get any worse, the news that Tay was pregnant reached Manny and my mother. Here I was, about to be sixteen years old, with two different pregnant girls.

Manny demanded that I stop talking to Tay and focus on the child I would have with his sister. He even went so far as to delete her number from my phone. Hating the way my mother and Manny started treating me, Jay purposely got his girlfriend pregnant to try to take some of the heat off me, but that didn't work. They just praised Jay and his baby mother as if his being two years older really made a difference.

Since I hadn't spoken to Tay in a few weeks, her mother called me, concerned, and asked what I wanted to do about the baby. Manny was there, his fist balled, ready to hit me if I didn't say what he wanted to hear. After I was forced to say I didn't want anything to do with the baby, Tay's mother did what she thought was best and took her fourteen-year-old daughter to get an abortion. I didn't find out until days later, when Tay called me during gym class because she couldn't participate. My heart broke, and I yearned to comfort her. Not only was she forced to go through this unwanted abortion, but she was also pregnant with twins. I had so much guilt built up that I blamed myself for not standing up to Manny. Now I had lost the set of twins I'd always wanted. It hurt, and I could only imagine the suffering Tay must have gone through, being there without me. Sadly, I never got the chance to truly apologize, as that was the last time I would speak with Tay.

A year passed, and Teela and I thought the birth of Dre Dre would change Manny's heart, but it did the opposite. I had just turned seventeen, and the abuse had reached its peak. Regardless of whether Manny was drunk or not, he was enraged all the time. He spent all day in the house, paranoid because he had violated his probation. By this time, my mother was fed up with Manny's vicious habits, and we continued to pray that God would open a door for us to escape. Because Manny was now on the run for some felony charges, I knew it was only a matter of time before we were free.

"Faith, help me find my damn keys!" Manny demanded.

"I'm looking," she said as she scavenged the counter.

"Keep talking back and see if I don't come over there and break your fucking jaw," Manny threatened.

What is his deal with breaking people's jaws? I wondered. If he hits my mom one more time, it'll be a miracle if I don't kill him! Although I was temporarily paralyzed with fear and anchored to the couch, I still had my mother's back.

"I see where your kids get it from," he continued. My mother knew to keep silent as she continued looking for his keys. When her phone rang, she stopped what she was doing and answered.

"Hey, mom," she greeted, knowing it was my Grandma Pumpkin by the caller ID. I was relieved because Manny always got his act together around her.

"BITCH, WHAT THE FUCK ARE YOU DOING?" Manny screamed at the top of his lungs.

"My mother called," was the only thing she could say before he charged at her.

"Bitch, I don't give a fuck. What did I say to do? Hang that shit up now!" Manny demanded. My mother didn't say bye; she just hung up. As soon as she put the phone down, Manny slapped my mother upside her head. I was furious, but I was still paralyzed and too afraid to move.

"Stop!" I finally built up the courage to speak.

"What the fuck you say?" Manny had now turned his attention toward me.

Taking advantage of the opportunity, my mother made a run for it. Shooting off like a sprinter, she unlocked the front door and was out of the house in a matter of seconds. Manny chased after her, but my mother refused to be captured. My siblings and I ran upstairs to look out the window—hoping he didn't catch her. I grabbed the phone and called the police while I ran back downstairs to lock him out.

"Hello? I need an officer at 4242 Madison Ridge right now. Please hurry! My mom's husband is about to beat her!" I begged her to rescue. "Please come help."

"Okay, calm down. Where is he now?" the operator asked.

"Outside, chasing her," I answered. I looked out the window and saw Manny banging on Mrs. Michelle's door. "She ran to her friend Mrs. Michelle's house, who lives five houses down on the right," I said, panicking.

"Lock all the doors so he doesn't get back in and stay on the phone with me until one of the officers arrives, okay?" the operator instructed for our safety. A few minutes later, a squad car turned the corner and stopped at our house as an officer got out.

"He's over there!" I yelled out the window. A few seconds later, another squad car turned the corner, followed by several others that went straight to Mrs. Michelle's house after being directed by the first officer. Once the cops spotted Manny, it took three officers to restrain him because of his strength and resistance.

"They got him! Thank you so much," I said before hanging up the phone.

When my mother finally came out of Mrs. Michelle's, she was surrounded by the 12 officers now at the scene. While one took down her statement, another drove Manny off to jail. The rest began taking pictures of my mother's body and the evidence in the house. For the first time in a while, I felt safe. Finally! I thought I could breathe again, but the look on my mother's face told me more trials and tribulations were ahead.

"Okay, guys, I need y'all to pack up your school clothes and a few more things you'd want to take," my mother directed my little brothers and sisters after she came inside from talking to the officers. At the time, Jay was in the Army, stationed in Georgia, so it was just us.

"Where are we going, mom?" I asked nervously.

"Look, Dre, I need to talk to you alone," she said. She waited for my little brothers and sisters to do as they were told while trying to find the courage to tell me what she was about to say. "I am finally getting some help. I can no longer allow you kids to suffer, let alone myself. I'm going to a shelter for abused women, honey."

A shelter for women? Well, count me in! I love women, I thought.

"I'm sorry, baby, but since you're seventeen… in Texas, they consider that an adult." Her voice was now shaking as she continued, "So in order for us to go, you won't be able to come with me."

A wrecking ball came crashing into my heart—shattering it into pieces. Here I was about to enter my senior year of high school, and now my family was splitting up. I should have been preparing for prom, college, and life after high school, but instead I had to focus on surviving. I hated and blamed Manny for ruining my life.

Feeling rejected, I cried out, "Mom, I don't want to be separated from my family!" My mind started running wild, and all I saw was me alone, surrounded by darkness.

## <u>*7. F.O.E (Friends Over Everything):*</u>

*"A friend loveth at all times, and a brother is born for adversity."*
**— Proverbs 17:17—**

"My Lord!" Mrs. Karolyn held her chest in shock. "Did he go to jail?"

"Yes, he ended up in prison, and my mother filed for divorce," I answered.

"Wait. Let's go back for a second," Mrs. Karolyn stopped me, as if she were rewinding my story in her mind. "Why didn't anyone go to the police before?"

"Where I'm from, we don't believe in calling the cops. Besides, they don't care about us anyway. I've seen my mother abused a few times and even had a gun put to her head by her baby daddy. What did the police do? Nothing! In fact, they let him out 3 days later without giving my mother a single notice," I said in anger, thinking back on the situation.

"So, did you tell Zion?" Mrs. Karolyn asked, switching the topic as she noticed the tension building in my body.

"Of course, I told Zion. I told him everything! But we both knew we were limited in what we could do because of the other siblings. I remember one day, while Manny was asleep on the couch, I passed by a hammer. My initial thought was to bash his skull in, but then I wondered if the hammer would even faze him. I also knew that if I did, one of the 12 siblings would surely kill my family or me."

"I can't imagine dealing with all that at such a young age. Were there any good times before Manny?" Mrs. Karolyn asked.

"Honestly, things were always up and down based on my mother's relationship status. Manny may have been the worst, but he was certainly not the only abuser my mother dated. For some reason, they all felt it was their place to mold me into their version of what a man should be, but I am thankful that my mother kept me in church and introduced me to my Heavenly Father."

"Growing up, everyone told me I had a calling on my life because I used to preach and recite Scripture. *I want to be just like Martin Luther King Jr,* I would tell the elders. I also loved going to church camps. If I'm being honest, it wasn't just for God; the girls were another big motivating factor. When I was fifteen, the youth members of my church went to Colorado. At that time, I had just remixed Yung Joc's song **It's Going Down** to **He's Coming Down** and decided to perform it at the talent show. When I performed the song, the whole church camp went crazy, even the adult counselors were into it. After the performances, we were supposed to join the rest of our church in the mountains for praise and worship. I really didn't want to go, so my friend and I tried to hide in the pool with the girls from the other churches. When we got caught, we were ordered to get out, get dressed, and join the rest of our church. Initially, I planned to tune everything out, but I was shocked when I saw everyone in tears, speaking in tongues, when we reconnected with our group. It scared me, but it also frustrated me, because I thought they were all faking. I really got mad when the same friend I was with at the pool caught the Holy Spirit. Noticing my frustration as I yelled at them to stop, my youth pastor approached me. He opened the Bible to Acts 2:12-18 and had me read about the crowd that laughed and ridiculed the people who caught the Holy Spirit in the street. It broke me down and made me realize I was just like those laughing in the Bible. That day, I learned that God could reach you wherever you are, but it's up to you to receive Him. The irony was that the message was in my song the whole time, meet me in the trap, He's coming down. Meet me in the mall. He's coming down. Meet me at the club, He's coming down; anywhere you're at, guaranteed He's coming down.' I recited the chorus to my song. At first, I wanted to change it to meet me at the church. He's coming down, but my youth pastor told me to just leave it alone because that would hit home with everyone. He reminded me that no matter who you are or where you are, God will meet you regardless of your circumstance." After reminiscing, I got back on topic.

"During those times when it was just us, life was great. My mother made sure we were always happy. We would have weekly game nights and monthly field trips. When she was single, she was the shit! But as I mentioned before, things always changed when my mother started dating yet another asshole. No more game nights, no more snacks, no new toys, and no more family functions. It felt as though my mother put her kids on the back burner to focus on her current boyfriend." I concluded.

"You mentioned before that you felt targeted by your mother's boyfriends. Why do you think they focused on you and not your other siblings?" Mrs. Karolyn asked curiously.

"To be real, it was probably because I was the worst out of my mother's six kids," I confessed. "I was always in trouble or giving my mother some type of hell by getting into something I wasn't supposed to, especially when we were in public. I don't know what it was about having an audience, but it always hyped me up. When my mother would pop me for doing something I had no business doing, I would flop on the floor like I was being abused. She hated taking me places as a child," I laughed—finding myself enjoying sharing stories with Mrs. Karolyn. "In 5th grade, I thought it was funny to get the lowest grade on my report card since everyone else was trying to get the highest. I achieved that goal by getting a 10. I remember proudly showing all my friends and thinking it was so funny. Now, I was far from dumb; I just lacked attention at home, so I tried to get it at school. Anyway, since Winter Break was starting that day, I made sure to add another zero, so I could spare myself a whooping. After thoroughly examining my new grade, I knew there was no way in hell my mother would buy it. Panicking, I made a last-minute decision to say that I left my report card at school. I figured if I could just buy myself some time, I'd have a wonderful Christmas and face the punishment afterward.

When I got home later, of course, the first thing my mother asked for was my report card. I stuck with my plan, not knowing she'd grab her car keys—prepared to drive down to the school. I decided to just try my luck and give her the altered paper. When she unfolded the report card, she immediately noticed the added zero. Of course, I told her my teacher made a mistake, after all, there was no way in hell I could get a 10, right? I lied so much back then that my mother never believed me, but she also didn't think I was dumb enough to get a 10 on my report card. She marched me up to that school, talked to my teacher, and found out not only that I deserved that 10, but also that he let her know I was a 'class clown, very disrespectful and disruptive in class all the time.' Mrs. Karolyn, when I say I was beat like Kunta Kinte, I am not lying. My mom used one of those thick black cable cords and tore my behind up. Oh, but that wasn't the worst part. After my lashing, she made me call each of my grandmas. The real punishment wasn't the whooping; it was confessing everything that I did and losing out on my Christmas gifts." I laughed so hard that tears were running down my cheeks.

*Wow, I haven't laughed since Zion…,* I sadly thought, still refusing to accept reality. Every bit of happiness was suddenly overpowered by my sadness, causing an internal shutdown once again. My body became numb as the guilt made my stomach sick.

"What's wrong, Dre?" Mrs. Karolyn asked, noticing the change in my demeanor. "One minute you're laughing, and I can start to see a glimpse of you pulling yourself out of your shell. Then, in the blink of an eye, it's like you lose your footing and fall back into a tunnel of—" she paused, lost for words. She then broke the silence, "I can't figure it out, because you display signs of anger, but then there's deep sadness. Or maybe it's something else. Whatever it is, I can see something is causing you great emotional turmoil. Do you know what it is?" She questioned. When I didn't respond, she looked deeply into my eyes—penetrating down to my soul and said, "Dre, please tell me more about Zion."

;

Zion just graduated from North Crowley High School and had a full-ride scholarship to the University of Oklahoma. He was so excited, and we all knew he was destined to make the Olympics. Unfortunately, he injured his hamstring in a fight, which led to the revocation of his scholarship. Zion was devastated. He wanted to follow in his parents' footsteps at OU, but instead, he spent all summer recovering from his injury and attended Tarrant County Community College in the fall.

I, on the other hand, just entered my senior year of high school, and the transition was smooth until Homecoming week. After one of the Showgirls informed me that they were dancing to "Gimme That," my homie G-Money and I came up with a plan to steal the show. When the song came on, we jumped out of our seats and started dancing and singing. We made our way down the aisle, pop-locking and Usher sliding, as the girls screamed at the top of their lungs. A teacher tried to stop me, but I took it as she wanted to have a dance battle. So, I hit her with my best moves; literally. Even though it wasn't intentional, I accidentally kicked her while I was Krump dancing. Unaware of what I just did, I kept going. I hopped onstage and really started to give the crowd a show as if I were Chris Brown himself. Everyone seemed to be enjoying it, except the Showgirls; they were pissed. Before the song ended, Principal Arnette turned the music off and escorted G-Money and I to his office. While we were both suspended for 3 days, he told me I wasn't allowed to go to the Homecoming game. Of course, I came up with the most brilliant plan to go anyway.

"You ready?" Zion asked, as we looked for a parking spot in his 1996 Pathfinder.

"Hell yeah!" I was excited about what was coming.

"Check your breath, because when you were talking earlier, it was fucking up my nostrils!" Zion joked. "You didn't notice me letting the windows down?"

We both laughed as I coughed up smoke from the blunt. We had just pulled up to Farrington Field, where Southwest held all their home games. Zion always loved making an entrance, and since I had plans to be the Halftime Show, our late arrival was perfect.

"You're hilarious," I said sarcastically. "But I know you're not talking! Your breath smells like 8 cans of shark shit." No matter what Zion fired at me, I was quick on my feet and always had something to fire back.

"Okay, this is my last time trying to talk some sense into yo dumb ass. Are you sure you want to do this?" Zion asked once again.

He always tried to talk me out of my foolishness, but I was too hot-headed. Besides, with everything going on with my mother and my living situation, I yearned to be the center of attention somewhere. The popularity made me feel like I mattered. Zion understood that, and no matter what stupid idea I came up with, he always had my back. This time was no different. Even though he knew better, he also knew there was no way to talk me out of running across the field during halftime.

"Yes, I'm sure! Watch, when I run across this field, everyone is gonna get crunk! This is about to be the greatest halftime show ever," I said confidently. "I'm going to be the first person to do something like this!"

"Bro, you just said your mother told you not to get into any more trouble. You literally got suspended earlier! But if you must, then as I said, I've got your back," Zion promised.

"I know, but my mom isn't here, is she? I'm out here by myself," I said.

"Nah, I'm here," Zion countered. "Don't forget I chose to leave my mother's house to look after you."

I couldn't argue with that. Zion was the realest person I ever knew. When he found out that Ms. Nicole's apartment was the only option I had to lay my head, he told me to ask if he could move in too. I begged her to let him stay, and when she agreed, he left his mother's two-story house to be a loyal friend. That alone was something I never expected from anyone, but the fact that he actually did it earned him my loyalty for life.

"You're right. So, since you're here, have my back!" I demanded.

"As you wish," Zion said—giving me the green light. He led the way as we walked through the gates of Farrington Field, passed through the security checkpoint, and made our way to the concession stand to link up with our clique.

"Yo, NiggaMan! Are you really going to do it?" my homie Bob asked, since everyone had heard about the plan.

"Is water wet?" I said sarcastically as a cop walked up to us.

"Y'all need to go sit down if you're not buying anything from the concession stand," the officer ordered.

We didn't budge; instead, we all turned our backs on him and resumed our conversation. I never understood why cops felt like they could tell everyone what to do just because they wore a badge. It's not like they had the power to create laws as they went.

"If you do not comply, I will call for backup, and we will escort all of you out of this stadium," the officer added.

"Where does it say we have to sit and watch the game?" I questioned. "Last time I checked, we paid to come in, so you can't just kick us out because we don't want to sit down. Besides, there are no rules written that say we must remain seated unless we are buying from the concession stand."

"It doesn't matter if it's written, I am an officer of the law!" he answered. "This is a fire hazard, so if I say go sit down because I feel it's safer, then you will obey or be forced to leave!"

"You're just scared because you see a group of black teenagers linked up and assume we're some type of threat," Zion told the officer.

"You! Come with me," the officer demanded while grabbing Zion by his arm. "Breaker breaker, I have a 426 in progress. I have one detained and am requesting backup by the east wing concession stand," the officer spoke into his walkie-talkie.

"I didn't do shit," Zion said in anger.

I immediately went into rage mode as I watched the officer's backup come and escort Zion out the gates. "Y'all weak! Always abusing your authority, but never helping when we really need you," I yelled at the cops.

"DRRREEEE!!!!" Zion screamed from the other side of the gate.

Before I could turn to see why he screamed, a strong arm wrapped around my neck and tightly squeezed. Struggling to release the air from my lungs, the officer started dragging me and threw me up against the gated fence. I never felt strength like that before. He then grabbed me by my throat and began choking me. He applied so much pressure that I started losing oxygen, making it hard to breathe.

"I …. can't……breathe!" I tried to get the words out as best I could.

"He can't breathe! GET OFF OF HIM!" I heard a female voice plead from the bystanders who were recording with their phones. My vision began to fade, and darkness took over.

Suddenly, out of my peripheral, I saw someone running fast as lightning—bulldozing into the officer who was choking me. When the officer released his grip, I struggled for a second to catch my breath. When my vision became clearer, I noticed it was Zion to my rescue once again. I attempted to get up and help him, but a mob of officers came and threw us to the ground. As they put handcuffs on us, they began to read us our Miranda Rights. I was pissed because *how the hell do you choke me out for talking and then arrest me?* Not only did they ruin my plans for the halftime show, but they also tried to slap us with charges we never committed.

It was the first time in my life that I had gotten arrested, but once again, I wasn't alone. Despite everything, I was thankful they put Zion and I in the same pod. Even though this was only his second time being arrested, Zion showed me the ropes of jail life and how to survive. I will admit, there's something about being in a cell that makes you reflect upon your life and choices. One thing I knew for sure was how blessed I was to have a friend like Zion by my side.

Although word quickly spread to my mother about our arrest, it took her a couple of days and several phone calls before she was able to piece everything together. After obtaining video footage, my mother went and raised hell at the police station. She threatened to send the video of their officers assaulting two unarmed black students to every news outlet in the city. Conveniently, they dropped all charges—hoping to prevent a lawsuit and the videos from going viral. When they finally released us from jail, my mother was there waiting to pick us up.

"MOM!" I hugged her tightly. Deep down, I was a mama's boy, and not seeing her these past weeks felt like a century. "How are you? How are my brothers and sisters? Have you talked to Jay? Have you been eating?" I purged all my questions while I continued to latch onto her—refusing to let go.

"Dang! Can I hug my mama too?" Zion teased as he went in for a hug after I finally released her. "Hey, Mama C, how are you and the kids?" Zion asked.

"Hey, son! They are good, but I'm more concerned about you two," my mother started.

"This may sound familiar, but this time it really wasn't our fault. So just forget all that. Tell me about y'all. Can I come with you now?" I asked, hopeful she'd say yes.

"Again, I'm fine, baby. So are your siblings, but—," she paused. "Jay went AWOL."

"WHAT!" I shouted. "Why?"

"After I told him what happened, he refused to stay at the base. He regrets leaving us and blames himself for not standing up to Manny. I don't know where he is, but I know he needs to go to Kentucky so he can be officially discharged. Otherwise, the military will be looking for him," my mother informed me. "All we can do is pray about that, but back to YOU!! What did I tell you about being on your best behavior? If Ms. Nicole kicks you out, you will have nowhere to go. I am still at the shelter, so coming with me right now isn't an option. Thankfully, the Landlord gave me another month to get all our stuff out of the old house, which is a blessing since we are still on the waitlist for housing assistance. So, hear me clearly. I need you to be on your best behavior. I don't want to worry about you being in these streets, in a jail cell, or worse. Do you understand me?"

"Yes, ma'am," I answered.

"Uh, hello," my mother nudged Zion. "I'm talking to you, too, son!"

"Yes, ma'am," Zion said respectfully.

My mother dropped us off at Ms. Nicole's apartment, thanked her again, and then headed back. Although the shelter had strict rules about leaving, they made an exception for her because I had been arrested. Ms. Nicole left shortly after my mother, heading to work. Before she left, she smoked with Zion and me and gave us some weed to smoke while she was gone.

The night felt like it came faster than usual, and I began to have the urge to smoke again.

"Yo Ace roll up!" I told Zion.

"We need a Swisher," Zion informed me.

"Let's mob to Kyrie's," I suggested.

Kyrie's was the hood store where everyone posted up and hung out. The owner, Kyrie, was the coolest guy I ever met. He had a studio at the gas station and a Church's Chicken, which he used to donate unsold food to the community. Growing up, we stole so much from the store that Kyrie quickly learned our names, and after talking to my mother, he built a relationship with us.

"Aight bet. You got the key?" Zion asked.

I searched my pockets, but to my surprise, they weren't there. I went to check in my dirty clothes basket, but no luck. "Damn, I can't find it," I admitted. "The store is literally across the street, though, let's just run there and back. Besides, Ms. Nicole won't even be home until the morning."

"Boy, did you not hear Mrs. Nicole's only rule? You are hardheaded! I see why you used to get your ass whooped all the time!" Zion laughed. Ms. Nicole had given us only one rule: always lock the door when we left, because she had a ten-year-old son.

"Bro, it's literally across the street! Aren't you the fastest nigga in Fort Worth? Come on and stop being a PUSS!" I enticed.

"Aight," Zion said, shaking his head. "But if we get kicked out, it's your fault."

"Bro, she's at work. C'mon, we're good."

We grabbed our black hoodies and headed across the street. As we got closer to the store, Zion recognized one of the guys posted up. From the look on Zion's face, I could tell we were about to fight.

"Yo NiggaMan, there goes that bitch ass nigga Joe right there!" Zion was still pissed about what happened a few weeks ago. Minutes after buying a pistol from Joe, a group of guys conveniently rushed in with their own guns drawn. Not only did they keep Zion's money, but they also demanded that he give them the pistol. Ever since then, Joe has been ducking Zion.

""He finally came out of hiding, I see," I said.

We put our hoods on, tightened the strings, and walked through the parking lot. When Joe separated from the group, Zion took his cue and went to confront him. Zion swung open the front doors of Kyries with so much force that everyone immediately stopped and turned toward him.

"Bring your bitch ass outside, pussy!" Zion shouted.

Refusing to look like a punk, Joe walked toward Zion nervously. Instead of sneaking up on Joe at the door, Zion held it open and waited for him to square up. That's another thing I respected about Zion; when he whooped your ass, he always did it like a man. He wouldn't stomp you, sneak up on you from behind, or pull out a weapon; he'd just give you a fair one.

After Joe posted up, he took a swing but missed. Zion countered with a haymaker, connecting straight to Joe's jaw—dropping him in his place. It was my first time seeing someone get knocked out in real life instead of in a movie. Soon after, Kyrie came running out of the store. Since he knew about my living situation and had promised my mother he'd look out for me, he told Zion and me to go lay low before the cops or Joe's friends came looking for us. Doing as we were told, Zion and I ran across the street, through the complex, and back to Ms. Nicole's apartment. To my surprise, the door was locked when I tried to open it.

"What the hell? I didn't lock it," I told Zion, puzzled.

Just when I was about to knock, the door unlocked from the inside. I was shocked when I saw Ms. Nicole standing there with fury in her eyes.

"What did I tell you? All I had was one fucking rule!" Ms. Nicole scorned. "My son! My precious son was asleep while you were out doing what? You better not tell me that was y'all over there fighting at the gas station either!"

"It's my fault. We ran to the store to grab a swisher, and since I couldn't find my key, we tried to make it fast," I hoped my honesty would get us out of trouble.

"You don't have your key because you left it in my car," she said, pulling it out of her pocket. "So, answer me this, was that you guys fighting or not?"

"Yes, ma'am," I answered truthfully. "But—"

"Ain't no buts! Now, I'm sorry. This really breaks my heart, but pack y'all shit. Y'all cannot stay here any longer. Y'all had my baby sleep on the couch, door unlocked all WHILE Y'ALL WERE FIGHTING!" At this point, she was practically shaking as she thought of what could have happened. "What if they followed you here? Or worse, what if y'all had gotten shot? I wouldn't have known shit and would've had to explain to your mothers! Nah, I can't have that on me. Y'all put my son and me in danger by fighting so close to where we lay our heads. That might have been cool at your mom's, but not here!" Ms. Nicole was beyond pissed. "I opened my door to you, Dre, when no one else would, and this is how you repay me?"

I sat there dumbfounded, not hearing anything else she said. Now, where the fuck am I gonna go? Damn, I should have just listened to Zion. While a million thoughts swirled through my mind, all I could say was "I understand. Thank you for letting us stay this long."

After Zion and I packed all our things, we started to head out, but Ms. Nicole stopped us and asked if we wanted to have one last session. We all sat on the couch silently, sunken in our thoughts. After we smoked our last blunt with Ms. Nicole, we thanked her again and left.

"Now, where to, my boy?" Zion asked.

"I guess let's go back to my momma's old crib and thug it out," I suggested.

"I'm down with that!" Zion said. "As long as we got each other and a blunt, we're straight."

Once again, Zion proved his loyalty by sticking by my side. I was beyond thankful not to be alone, and I knew, no matter what, we would be friends forever.

## *8. Uprooting:*

*"He also brought me up out of a horrible pit, out of the miry clay, and set my feet upon a rock, and established my steps."*—**Psalm 40:2**—

The guilt of Zion being in this predicament ate me up inside, but no matter how many times I told him to just go home, he refused. Zion insisted that we were in this together. After our 3-mile walk, I was thankful when we arrived at my old house because the beds were still there. Sadly, there was no food or electricity. After settling into my old room and putting my things up the way I had them before, I walked downstairs to a perfectly rolled blunt.

"Ready to smoke?" Zion asked.

"Yeah," I said. "I know I apologized before, but I'm sorry I didn't listen and got us kicked out."

"We can't change the past, so we might as well focus on what lies ahead. This life is chess, not checkers! You must quickly adapt and focus on your next move," Zion said as he lit the blunt. "Speaking of next moves, we need a plan to come up with some money, fast."

"Now you sound like Manny with that dumb shit, 'life is like chess, not checkers.' Nigga, life is like a box of chocolates; you never know what you're going to get," I said, impersonating Forrest Gump.

"Well, if he was saying stuff like that, then maybe he wasn't all that bad. Don't miss the message because of the messenger," Zion lectured.

"Forget all that. He was the biggest hypocrite I've ever met! How is he going to tell me not to disrespect my mother because I only get one in this life, then minutes later beat the hell out of her in front of me? I don't respect anything that came out of that man's mouth," I said as my anger began to resurface.

"I can understand that, but all I'm saying is you don't know everything he's been through. Remember, God can use anyone."

I loved talking to Zion because he made you look at things from all angles. He was straightforward and honest, but sometimes in life, we can't handle the truth.

"No funny business, but I love you, fam. Thanks for thuggin' it out with your boy."

"Ah, shit, you not about to start crying, are you?" Zion asked, laughing. "Real talk, I love you too. You're like a little brother to me, so I'm always gonna have your back."

Suddenly, there was a loud, aggressive knock at the door.

"Who the hell is that? No one even knows we're here," Zion whispered.

"How the hell am I supposed to know?" I whispered back. I looked through the peephole and saw it was my homie, Deshawn.

"Wassup, man? Why are you banging on my door like you're the police?" I asked Deshawn after opening the door. "How did you even know I was here?"

"When I heard about Zion's fight, I figured y'all would come here to lay low. You ain't hear?" Deshawn asked, puzzled.

"Hear what?" I asked curiously.

"Joe came back looking for y'all! He was three cars deep, and all of them were strapped. The block got so hot, Kyrie had to close the store early because they refused to leave," he informed.

"Well, come inside then," I rushed him in. I locked the door and looked out the front window—making sure he hadn't been followed. After the coast was clear, we went to join Zion in the kitchen.

"It never fails! Deshawn always comes around right when we spark a blunt," Zion said right on cue. "Boy, your Spidey senses must tingle for Mary Jane!"

"I see this is what I get for looking out for the homies," Deshawn said. "So, it's just y'all here? Why are the lights off? Let me find out y'all didn't pay the bill."

"That's another story I got to catch you up on, but basically this is a Vacco," I answered.

"For real? Bro, let me stay here with y'all. I can turn the lights on right now," Deshawn pleaded.

"Swear? If you can get these lights on, then hell yeah, you can stay," I answered.

"Aight bet! I just need one of y'all to hold up a light by the meter, so I don't electrocute myself," Deshawn requested.

"I'll go, because I got to see this!" I said, amused.

"Shit, me too!" Zion chimed in.

We all walked to the side of the house where the electric meter was located. Deshawn removed the cover and pulled off two plastic pieces. After messing with them, he put the cover back on and said he was done. I didn't believe him, so I ran inside. Sure enough, the electricity was on and the A/C was blowing.

"Who the hell taught you that?" I asked Deshawn, impressed.

"After my stepdad kicked me out, I had no other choice but to bounce between vacant houses and apartments. I had to learn quickly how to adapt in these streets so I could survive," Deshawn answered.

"What did I just say?" Zion said, elbowing me.

The next few weeks felt like a marathon of survival of the fittest. We knew getting jobs would make things easier, but no one called us back about the applications we put in. We needed money fast because staying at the house wouldn't be an option much longer. After our last run-in with the law, Zion was adamant about not going back to jail a 3rd time, so most of the moves Deshawn and I made for cash were just the two of us.

He may not have been the sharpest tool in the box, but Deshawn showed me how to break into just about every kind of car without the alarms going off. One night we struck gold when we found a 12-gauge shotgun, but we quickly realized that breaking into cars wasn't getting us anywhere. As days went by, we began to feel the desperation of hunger, which is exactly how Deshawn and I were able to talk Zion into a store run. We came up with a plan for who would get what, so we would have enough food for a few days. When we got back, Zion was the first to empty his backpack—pulling out two loaves of bread, five bags of chips, crackers, and some soup.

"What did you get?" Zion asked me.

"I just got burritos, hot pockets, and some sandwich meats," I answered. "What'd you get, Deshawn?"

Deshawn poured out his backpack, and a bunch of candy fell out, along with a bottle of wine.

"Man, what the hell? You stole nothing but candy?" Zion shouted in disbelief. "How are we going to survive on that?"

"Well, I knew y'all would grab what we needed, so I wanted to be different and get some candy," Deshawn answered foolishly.

The loud sound of a truck backing up interrupted our conversation. We went outside to make sure it wasn't the Constable coming to kick us out. To our surprise, it was a U-Haul driven by one of our new neighbors who was moving in.

"Wassup, neighbor?" I greeted him as he got out of the truck.

"Peace and love, brother. Howdy, I'm Billy," the neighbor introduced himself. "Is that pot?"

"Yeah, you want to smoke?" I offered.

"Hell yeah, brother! I thought you'd never ask," Billy said as he came over. I gave him the blunt, and he immediately coughed after his first hit.

"If you like that, I can get you some for the low," I said, trying to hustle.

"No offense, buddy, but I know the difference between good shit and Reggie. Besides, my brother sells Dro. So, if y'all want some top-shelf quality, let me know. I'm sure we can work out some kind of neighbor discount, especially if y'all helped us build our clientele while we're at the oil rig," Billy propositioned. "Since we're not from around here, and y'all are familiar with the area. We could use your street smarts.

"Oh, word? How much for an ounce?" Zion questioned.

"Well, what we have is rare. Nobody on the street has this, so we can sell it at any price. I'll talk to my brother, though, and see if we can cut you a deal. Thanks for the smoke, but I'd better get back to it," Billy said as he continued unloading.

As we walked back into the house, Zion came up with the idea of using the neighbors as our "plug" to help with our money-making mission. We went along with his plan for a little while, but once we realized we were only making a few hundred dollars a week, we knew we had to change directions. When the Constable didn't come at the end of the month to clear out the rest of my mom's stuff, we knew our time was limited. So, Deshawn and I decided we would rob the neighbors' house that weekend, when they were back at the oil rig.

Early Saturday morning, we woke to the sound of the neighbors' Dually trucks starting. We knew today would be the day. We went over the game plan in my mother's bedroom because it had the best view of them leaving. About 20 minutes later, the garage opened, and a car backed out with a female driver. It's now or never! I thought.

"So, wait, you guys actually robbed them?" Mrs. Karolyn asked, snapping me back into my session. "I thought Zion was reluctant to do anything that would put y'all back in jail?"

"He was! He only agreed to help if he could be the lookout."

"So, what happened with the neighbors?" Mrs. Karolyn asked.

"They never said anything directly to us, and we didn't bring it up either. However, I'm pretty sure they figured it out when they came back and found all their weed gone. Besides that, an obvious clue, we stopped buying from them, and our house literally became the trap house next door. Two weeks after we stole all their weed, our spot was broken into while we were out. The next day, the

Constable came to make us leave, which I'm pretty sure the neighbors had something to do with that complaint.

"You have lived an interesting life, I see. I appreciate you sharing these colorful memories, for lack of better words, but prepare yourself. I want to focus specifically on what you have been avoiding talking about. So, go home and I want you to think about that night. If you're ever going to heal, we need to dig deeper and pull up the roots. Tomorrow, I want to know more about what happened to Zion," Ms. Karolyn said firmly.

I drove home in silence, trapped in my thoughts. I wanted to be open with Mrs. Karolyn, but after everything I've been through, trusting someone is hard for me. I knew Tam could help me figure out what to say, so I tried to call her to tell her about my session, but she didn't answer. I tried again and again. Still, she didn't pick up. I became agitated, wondering why in the hell she wasn't answering, because she knows I hate it when my calls are ignored. With my mind tormenting me, I drove faster, trying to get home. When I finally made it, I stormed into the apartment—slamming the door behind me. I didn't see Tam, but I could hear her upstairs.

"WHY ARE YOU IGNORING ME?" I yelled as I walked into the bathroom. "What's the point of me paying your phone bill if you're not going to answer?"

"What are you talking about?" Tam responded, confused about where my aggression was coming from. "Clearly, I'm bathing Zion, and before that I was feeding him. Plus, my phone is on the charger."

"Yeah, right. I don't smell any food. What were you really doing, Tam? Cheating?"

"Woah! Okay, I don't know why you're mad or what happened in your therapy session, but please calm down. I hate it when you yell in front of our son," Tam said.

"You think I care! You're on your phone 24/7, but the minute I leave and try to call, you conveniently don't answer?"

Tam grabbed Zion and tried to walk away to avoid a fight, but I followed her downstairs. I pressed all her buttons until she finally gave me what I seemed to want: an argument.

"Ok, Manny!" Tam said to piss me off. "That's exactly who you act like when you're mad!"

"Bitch, what did I tell you about calling me that?" I yelled as I walked up to her with my fist balled, just like Manny used to do with my mom.

"What are you going to do? Hit me, Manny?" Tam taunted.

"I'm not fucking Manny!" I screamed as I punched the wall in anger.

"I can't believe you just put another hole in the wall. That's it! I'm leaving and going to your mom's house. I can't stand it when you're like this," Tam said as she walked out.

The sound of the door slamming brought me back to my senses, and I immediately felt remorseful. No matter how much I wanted to deny it, I was becoming just like Manny. I knew that Tam not answering the phone wasn't the real issue. If I'm being honest, all this therapy—reliving memories and talking about Zion really had triggered me.

I didn't wake up to breakfast the next morning, indicating Tam was still mad. I felt bad, but I knew an apology wouldn't be enough this time. The guilt returned, and I could only imagine my mother's face while hearing that the very son who witnessed her struggles was becoming more and more like her abuser. I got tired of beating myself up, so I threw on some clothes and went to therapy. When I got into Mrs. Karolyn's office, my mind was still on Tam.

"What's wrong?" Mrs. Karolyn asked, reading the emotions on my face.

"Nothing," I lied.

"Clearly there's something," she said. "Close your eyes and take a few deep breaths." I followed her orders, and by the fifth deep breath, I felt a little more relaxed. "Now what's wrong?" Mrs. Karolyn asked again.

"Last night, my wife and I got into it," I admitted. "I don't even know what it was about, honestly. All I know is, I was so mad that I lost control. When I finally calmed down and saw myself in the mirror, I saw Manny, which only made things worse."

"Dre, I hope you know that's not uncommon. Many people grow up and exhibit the same behavioral patterns as the adults who raised them. You saw a lot of aggressive men, so it makes sense that you are inclined to do some of what you saw when you're angry. One thing I've learned from both my personal and professional life is that you can only control the controllables. I know if you could, you would, but you can't change what happened yesterday. Unfortunately, we can't rewind the hand of time, which is why life is about learning from your mistakes and changing your behavior to prevent repeating the same offense. While you may be conditioned to certain ways, that doesn't mean you have to accept them permanently. Just like when you're watching tv, if a show comes on that you don't like, you can change it. Life is the same way! You can take action by changing your behavior or leaving that environment altogether." She then paused, "My hope is that through our sessions, you will be freed from any looming destructive behavior or guilt that remains. Let's take your mind off last night for a second and continue talking about Zion." She then looked me directly in my eyes and said, "Dre, tell me about that night."

I was caught off guard. *Oh my God, why do I have to tell her now? I didn't even smoke today,* I thought as my emotions started running wild. I stared at her, unsure if I was ready to talk about it.

Mrs. Karolyn then squeezed my hands and said, "Remember, I am here. Don't feel like you are facing these demons alone. God told the devil, 'GET BEHIND ME, SATAN!'"

The lack of weed in my system prevented me from masking my feelings. Everything started pouring out. "I'm sorry. I am so sorry!"

"Sorry for what?" Mrs. Karolyn asked.

"It's…all….my…fault," I muttered between sobs. I sat there feeling guilty and alone. Normally, I would try to run away from my problems, but this time I couldn't even find the strength. I sat there defeated as I wept.

"Dre, close your eyes and take three deep breaths," Mrs. Karolyn requested again.

I repeated the process, but this time it failed. The tears poured harder as the pain became too much.

"I know it feels like too much, but every storm has a calm center. Keep your eyes closed and continue to breathe as you try to find that center," Mrs. Karolyn directed. "Why are you sorry, Dre?"

Although it never ceased, the pain stopped long enough for me to talk.

;

A couple of months went by, and despite us still being homeless, it felt like things were beginning to move in our favor. We finally had enough money saved for an apartment, and I had just gotten an overnight stocking job at Walmart. We also learned from Zion's cousin that the military had a buddy system, which would allow us to go through the whole process together. Zion and I saw it as an opportunity to travel and make some money, but Deshawn didn't even consider it. Probably because he'd have to follow orders, which we all knew wasn't his strong point. Instead, he took the easy route and moved back in with his mother and stepdad.

After Zion and I visited a recruiting station, we decided to go with the Army route. The first step was to obtain my G.E.D., since I hadn't graduated yet. After that, our recruiter, Sgt. Jones, helped us with the enrollment process and set up the ASVAB test, which we passed. We were one step away from being enlisted; all we had to do was stop smoking. As easy as it sounds, that was the hardest part because weed was the only thing that gave me comfort, given the circumstances.

During this time, my mother was still in the shelter awaiting permanent housing. Even though Jay was back and had a big rental property, it was at capacity with his baby momma, two kids, and my little brother Toni living there with him. Zion and I knew that the two of us staying with either of them wasn't an option. While we waited for our next drug test, we decided to speak to an apartment manager about our situation with the Army and asked what was required to rent month-to-month. She informed us that all we needed was employment verification, which my manager signed later that night during my shift.

When I got off, I went back to the vaco to pack our stuff. Since it was still early, Zion was asleep, so I decided to take a quick nap too. Shortly thereafter, I was woken up by the police. I spent three hours in a holding cell before an officer finally came to speak to me. I thought that if I told him about my mother's situation and how it had led to me being homeless, he would show me some compassion, but that was not the case. I even told him I was going to the Army soon, but he didn't care. Instead of showing compassion, he threw breaking and entering charges at me and basically told me to plan to be there for a while. A few more hours went by, and to my surprise, I was told I had made bond. I didn't know who had bonded me out, but I figured it had to be my mother again. After signing some forms, I was escorted through the release exit for inmates. When the sliding door opened, I was shocked to see Zion standing there smiling.

"BRROOOO!" I yelled.

"AAAAAYYYEEEEE!" Zion shouted. "Why are you acting all surprised like I wasn't going to get my bro out? Besides, we have a future to achieve. You know I can't go to the Army without my NiggaMan."

"How the hell did you even get away?" I asked as I dapped him up.

"Man, it was crazy. I tried to wake you up multiple times, but as soon as I heard them enter the house, I jumped out the window," Zion explained.

"Damn, I was knocked out from that graveyard shift! Shoot, thanks for coming to bond me out," I laughed as I envisioned everything. "Wait, you didn't use the deposit money, did you? I didn't even get to tell you the news. My manager signed the verification form, so we can move into our own spot now."

"Nah, I still have the money," Zion assured. "Actually, it was this snow bunny I met named Vickie. Come on, let me introduce you to her."

We walked toward a black Honda Accord and were greeted by a white, blond-haired chick. Instantly, I didn't like her. She was one of those white girls who tried so hard to be black, but since she gave Zion the money, I kept my thoughts to myself. Besides, it was clear Zion macked his way into her bank account because he had her stop and buy me over $200 worth of clothes and hygiene products from Walmart. My mother used to warn me about thirsty girls like her and the trouble they brought, so I definitely had my guard up and eyes open.

After getting food, Vickie drove us to the suburbs where her grandmother stayed. We pulled into a long driveway that led to a big house. When she parked the car, she told us to stay put while she checked whether her grandma was sleeping. I took the opportunity to talk to Zion in private.

"Fam, I get that you're using this chick for her money, but I don't trust her," I told Zion. "Something doesn't sit right with me. I just got out of jail, and I'm not trying to go back. I mean, come on; she's clearly sneaking us into this old white woman's house."

"You're too paranoid, bro. Let's just save our money and ride this wave," Zion said. "Why pay rent in the hood when we can live here for free where it's good? Besides, we'll be going to the Army soon, so let's just have a little fun."

Zion made a good point. I decided to have his back the way he's always had mine, but I still had a bad vibe about her. Five days in, and my intuition proved correct. Vickie was exactly what I thought she was, an attention-seeking whore who maxed out her poor grandmother's credit card. Every day thereafter, I tried to convince Zion to get our own apartment, but he was adamant about staying there until the Army called.

One day, on the way back to Vickie's grandma's house, I got a frantic call from my little brother, Toni. He was screaming through the phone—telling me to come help him because some dudes were trying to jump him. I couldn't really understand it all, but once he said he was at Main Event, Zion hit a U-turn and sped in that direction. When we got there, we quickly located Toni inside and got more details. After I learned that it was my homie's little cousins, I thought I'd be able to squash it with a conversation. Clearly, I was wrong because when Zion and I approached them, things quickly escalated. Getting tired of the back-and-forth, Zion told them to come outside so that we could fight. Knowing they didn't stand a chance, they retreated but promised to catch each of us slipping.

"What happened?" Mrs. Karolyn asked, once again snapping me out of my memory.

"Well, that's basically how I got my felony. After everything died down, we took Toni home, and I went to work. Coincidentally, the dudes just happened to walk in seven deep.

While I was helping a customer, they saw me and rushed me. I wanted to run, but since I was in an aisle, I was trapped as they came at me from both directions. I did all I could. I put my back against the shelves and tried to fight them off as best I could, but there were too many of them. Seeing this, one of my coworkers ran to get security. When the guys were satisfied, they tried to run, but I was so enraged that I hunted one down and started wailing on him. By the time security arrived, he thought I was the aggressor and cuffed me. Thankfully, the customer I was helping happened to be a lawyer and gave them a statement in my defense.

"But I thought your charge was for aggravated assault with a deadly weapon?" Mrs. Karolyn questioned.

"It is, but that wasn't the incident. After the lawyer told security what happened, they uncuffed me and tried to get me to snitch on who it was that jumped me. I didn't say a word; I was plotting in my head what I was going to do when I caught up to them. What really set me off was when the manager told me that he had to let me go, as if I had asked to be jumped at work. At that point, I was ready for war, so I called Zion to come get me," I said.

"What did Zion do?"

"The look he gave me when he saw the knot on my head told me we were in agreement about what had to be done. We drove around looking for them all night, to no avail. Thanks to a little help, the next morning we drove straight to their neighborhood and waited. Once I recognized one of the guys who came out of the house, it was on. We pulled up, popped the truck, and fired off multiple rounds in broad daylight. After we emptied the clip, we sped off only to be halted at a red light. Then the weirdest thing happened: a cop drove right past us like he didn't hear anything. I told Vickie to drive normally while we headed to her grandmother's house to hide the guns. After that, we tried to go to Dallas for an alibi, but unfortunately, we never made it," I told Mrs. Karolyn as my body cringed from the muscle memory.

Shattered glass, thick black smoke, the pungent smell of gasoline, blaring sirens with more approaching, and excruciating pain down my spine as I levitated. I tried to speak, but the only thing that came out was the blood I spit up.

"What… happened?" I barely got out the words.

"Sir, you were hit by an 18-wheeler," the paramedic informed me before I blacked out.

## *9. Turning Point:*

*"And we know that in all things God works for the good of those who love him, who have been called according to his purpose."*

**—Romans 8:28 – "**

"Is that how Zion died?" Mrs. Karolyn asked on the edge of her seat.

"Hell no! He didn't have a scratch on him, but we both knew that crash was our karma for the shooting that had occurred less than 20 minutes prior. When the cops arrived at the scene, they saw the box of shotgun shells, which is how we became suspects in their investigation. Well, that, along with 4 witness statements. They put two and two together, which resulted in us being charged with five counts of aggravated assault with a deadly weapon," I answered.

"FIVE!? Five counts of aggravated assault? Are you serious, Dre?" Mrs. Karolyn asked. "Was anyone harmed?"

"Yes, ma'am, five counts," I said remorsefully. "Luckily, nobody was harmed, thank God. I don't think I could live with myself if I took someone's life."

"So, what happened to going to the Army?" Mrs. Karolyn questioned.

"Funny thing," I chuckled. "So, after the shooting, we stopped smoking and completed all the requirements to begin the enlistment process. Believe it or not, we wanted to change our lives for the better. The day before diagnostics, which was also the day before heading to boot camp, cops arrested Zion. Ironically, I only knew about it because his girlfriend called me crying. Initially, I didn't believe her, because I had just spoken with Zion 5 minutes earlier and everything was fine. Fearing they had a warrant for me too, I hid at my pregnant girlfriend's house and came up with a plan. I knew if I could just make it to my recruiter, I'd be safe by the next morning. Thankfully, I did, but my dumb ass wanted some spending money for the army base, so I convinced him to take me to Walmart to pick up my last check. When I got there, the manager told me to wait, but I had a weird feeling that something wasn't right. I made an excuse to go to the bathroom, and that's when I heard my name on the security radio. Not wanting to take any chances, I tried to leave quickly, but by the time I reached the exit, I was ambushed by what felt like a million cops. I told them they had the wrong guy until they showed me five different papers with the same old mug shot of me. I laughed.

"Was that when you served a year in the county?" Mrs. Karolyn asked.

"Yes, ma'am. I spent a year fighting my case, but I also used the time to get closer to God. I know it was God who blessed me with 10 years of probation, because the original offers were 20 to 30 years in prison. He knew I couldn't handle that time at 18. Hell, I couldn't even handle the year in the county alone. Thankfully, I didn't have to, though, because once again, Zion was there to get me through it. After his mother bonded him out, he continued to support me. Although my mom came to see me whenever she could, it was Zion who consistently lifted my spirits with his letters. He even let me call his mother's house collect so I could speak with my girlfriend or mother on a 3-way call. Since we had the same bond amount, $37,500, Zion told me he had a plan to get me out. He was going to grow and sell weed, since he knew my family couldn't afford to contribute much. The fact that he was the only one trying to help my family scrape up the money really showed me his loyalty. He could have left me stranded in there, but instead, he did everything in his power to make it more tolerable. I appreciated him so much for that, but I couldn't help but laugh, thinking about how much weed he'd have to grow and sell."

"Wow, I can see he was a loyal friend. You mentioned your girlfriend. I'm assuming she had the baby while you were incarcerated?" Mrs. Karolyn asked.

"While I was locked up, I got what they call a "Dear John" letter, letting me know the child wasn't mine and that she was sorry for dragging me along for 6 months. That killed my spirits, but I never questioned God."

"Then what happened?" Ms. Karolyn asked, deeply engaged.

After serving just over a year, I faced my final court date before the prosecutor took the case to trial. I stayed awake all night praying. When I arrived at court, God answered my prayers with a sentence of 10 years' probation. My lawyer was even surprised, since the previous offer was 25 years in prison. I made a promise to myself to follow a new path. After I was released, Zion and I dedicated our lives to God and began working at a rock mine. Around that time, I met Evette and quickly fell for her — so much so that I still have her name tattooed on my chest," I shared with Mrs. Karolyn.

"Wait a second. You're married, but you have another woman's name tattooed on your chest?" Clearly, Mrs. Karolyn was confused by my wife's audacity in even allowing such a thing.

"Yes, ma'am. Evette was my gutta chick. I called her that because where I'm from, it basically meant she was loyal and down for me. She was so beautiful, but she had a hood mentality. We met at the County Jail; she was visiting her baby daddy, and I was visiting my brother. During that time, I was staying with my mother, who finally got housing, but let's just say my mother and I get along better when I am not under her roof. Anyway, I went to visit my brother one day and overheard Evette going in on her baby daddy. Apparently, he fucked up and got caught cheating, which made it easy for me to slide into the picture. Evette let me move in with her and got me on my feet. She put clothes on my back and even gave me a car to drive. We were supposed to get married, but—" I stopped as the thought resurfaced.

"What happened?" Mrs. Karolyn asked, looking puzzled.

"Zion," I paused, trying to find the words that I still refused to accept. "Zion, um..." No matter how hard I tried, I just couldn't finish the sentence. "I lost my mind, okay?" I confessed.

The guilt consumed me as the memories flashed before my eyes. *I'm so sorry, Zion! This is all my fault; I know it. Your life was taken because of me. I will never forgive myself. If only I could trade places with you, I would, because you didn't deserve to die,* I wept.

"Dre?" Mrs. Karolyn called out as she grabbed my hand to comfort me in my brokenness. "How did Zion die?" Mrs. Karolyn asked in a soft, soothing voice that made me drift off into memory.

;

Evette and I were madly in love, and my life instantly changed because of her. I went from being homeless and not knowing where my next meal would come from, to living in a warm-loving home filled with lots of food. It was the first time I felt like I had someone who genuinely loved me and wanted the best for my future. Aside from wanting me to feel good, she pushed me to get my driver's license and treated Dre Dre like her own two little boys. We made a good team and when I wasn't working, I watched all three boys while maintaining the house. Zion didn't like the situation, and every time he came over, he would call me "Jefferey" from The Fresh Prince of Bel-Air. I would just laugh it off. *After all my struggles, I have everything I dreamed of; life is perfect!* I thought.

At that time, Zion was living with a friend because part of the stipulations of our probation was that we were not allowed to contact one another. Of course, that didn't stop us. Since the Army was no longer an option, we decided to enroll at Tarrant County Community College. Zion said we were going to treat this probation like a 10-year plan for our success, and getting a degree was the first step. Although we didn't have any classes together, we met up every day just to check up on each other. knowing the risks of getting into trouble, Zion was determined to ensure we both completed our probation successfully. This included paying our fees, abstaining from smoking, and attending weekly anger management classes. Things seemed to be going well, until I received another life-altering call.

"JOE TRIED TO KILL ME!" Zion shouted.

"Hell nah, where you at?" I asked, grabbing my strap. This was the second time this week he had come after Zion, and I was going to make sure it was the last. After I told Evette what happened, she agreed it was best for Zion to move in with us so I could have his back.

As I raced down I-20 to the Southwest side of town, a million thoughts flooded my mind. I swear, if Joe is still around, I'm going to end him, I thought as I pulled up. Once I located Zion, I told him we were going to find Joe.

"As much as I want revenge, I'm not trying to lose our freedom nor our lives!" Zion said.

I couldn't argue with that, and once again, Zion was the voice of reason. While some people may have only known him for getting into fights, I knew him for his character. On many occasions, he attempted to walk away, but this is Fort Worth; ain't no walking away!

As we hopped in the car, Zion opened up, "I appreciate you for coming to get me and y'all taking me in."

"Of course! You have always had my back, so it's only right that I show up for you. Besides, this is exactly how I wanted it."

"Speaking of that, do you have a toothbrush? Cuz man, you got a serious case of exactlies," Zion said.

"Exactlies?" I questioned.

"Yeah, that's where your breath smells exactly like your ASS!!" Zion couldn't contain his annoying laughter.

A couple of weeks went by, and I thought everything was going smoothly until I got a text message from Evette saying we needed to talk. My mind was racing while I waited for her to get home. Oh Lord, what is this about? I thought. Could she be pregnant? When she finally got home, I had a bubble bath waiting for her—hoping that might butter her up if it was bad news.

"Before you say anything, I made you a bubble bath," I blurted out when she walked in.

"Dre," she said as she slowly approached me. "I'm sorry, but the only way to say this is to be real. My baby daddy might be getting out, and honestly, I don't know if we're going to get back together or not," Evette said, as her words crushed me.

Get back together? I got your name tatted on my fucking chest, I thought. I was hurt, but more pissed off because how could she make me look so stupid?

"I'm sorry, Dre. I don't want to hurt you, but I don't know how I feel because he's the father of my kids. I am not saying you have to leave, though! You can stay here as long as you need," Evette said as she attempted to grab my hand.

"What? You must be out of your rabbit-ass mind if you think I am going to stay here. Let alone associate with you anymore. You said you loved me, but this is how you show it? We got each other's names tatted! For WHAT??" I shouted. "Forget it, I'll get my stuff later. I'm gone," I said as I passed her. I walked out the front door and noticed Zion smoking a cigarette on the stairs, so I went to join him.

"Let me hit that cuz," I told Zion.

"You good, bro?" Zion asked, noticing my demeanor.

"No! Evette wants to break up because her baby daddy is getting out."

"See! I told yo dumb ass and now look at you! Stuck with her name branded on you for life," Zion laughed, rubbing in the pain.

"You ain't funny! Now we need to find another place to stay, because I refuse to be around her. Can you believe she said she wants me to stay there until he's out?" I asked, taking another puff of the cigarette before passing it back.

"She still wants that ham," Zion joked. We both laughed, which made me feel somewhat better. That was one of Zion's gifts; he used humor to ease the pain. As we were talking, Jerome and Jerold walked up and pulled out a blunt. Ever since we helped them move into their apartment a few weeks ago, we've been cool with them.

"Y'all wanna smoke?" Jerome offered.

"Nah, we're good! We're on 10 years' probation," Zion answered for both of us. As we all sat, I told them what happened with Evette and I. Feeling bad, they offered to let us stay with them until we saved up for our own spot. Of course, we accepted, knowing we had no other options. As we were working out the details, we noticed a group of women coming up the stairs.

"Oh shit, there they go," Jerold said.

"Who are they?" Zion asked.

"They live next door to us. The ringleader, Tam, owns the apartment, but there are like four other chicks that stay there too," Jerome said.

I watched the women make their way toward us. I looked them over and stopped when I spotted the dark chocolate one with the long, black, silky hair. Who is that? I thought, admiring her from afar. When they reached the end of the stairs, they stopped.

"Now I know y'all seen us coming. Real gentlemen would have gotten up without having to be asked," the dark chocolate one said.

"Ashley?" Zion interrupted. "Girl, what are you doing here?" Zion asked, recognizing an old friend from high school.

"Zion? Boy, I thought that was yo crazy ass. How you been?" Ashley asked.

"Oh, I'm much better now. Lord! Can I get an amen, sista?" Zion joked, causing the other girls to laugh.

"Amen! I think I'm going to need you to come to my room and place those holy hands all over me," Ashley said as she grabbed Zion's hand, leading him up the stairs and into their apartment.

"Well, damn you, FREAK!" My crush yelled at Ashley. "Anyway, who are you?" She asked me.

"I'm NiggaMan," I answered.

"Boy, I know yo mama didn't name you that, and I sure as hell ain't calling you that," she said. What's your real name?"

"My government name? Why didn't you just say that?" I teased. "I'm Dre."

Tam rolled her eyes, giving me a cute, seductive smile that revealed her dimples. I could feel the sparks flying between us. "I'm Tamera, but everyone calls me Tam," she introduced herself.

"Nice to meet you, gorgeous."

"Nice to meet you, too, handsome. You got some good hair! What are you mixed with, Creole?" Tam asked as she touched my hair.

"Puerto Rican and Black." I lied, knowing most girls loved exotic men. I was really mixed with Finnish and Nigerian, but being labeled as 'black and white' didn't sound as cool.

"Why? You know how to braid?" I asked.

"Follow me," was all Tam said as she led everyone into her apartment and did my hair for the first time.

Jerome and Jerold were in awe of how quickly we got cool with their next-door neighbors. Apparently, they had been trying to talk to them for a while, but Tam's crew never seemed interested. A couple of weeks passed, and Zion and I spent a lot of time at Tam's. She was really cool; she would always cook for us, make us alcoholic drinks, and cater to our every need. She became a good friend and even told us that she was pregnant, instead of trying to hide it. Since her sperm donor left as soon as he got the news, Zion and I promised to take on uncle roles for the child. My feelings started to change, but as much as I liked Tam, I couldn't see myself dating a woman who was pregnant with another man's child.

We kept going back between that place and Jerome and Jerold's until one day, my shoes and Zion's wallet disappeared. When they returned our belongings and told their wild story, we lost trust in them. We quickly packed up and went to Tam's. She laughed at their story and said she didn't trust them either. She shared how they used to bother her—being childish and doing anything to get attention.

"You know you all can live here if you want?" Tam offered.

"Really?" Zion asked to confirm she wasn't joking.

"Yeah! I appreciate how y'all take out the trash, help with dishes, keep us laughing, and make us feel safe," Tam said. "Plus, you don't need to worry about theft here because nobody wants your beat-up Air Force Ones," Tam joked.

"Hell yeah! They look like he got them from a power line," Zion added, never missing a chance to roast.

"I know Brother Darkness isn't trying to high side," I told Zion.

"Aye, she said it, not me! I was just describing them," Zion joked.

Evette quickly found out I moved in with Tam and a place full of women. One day, while we were all playing Spades in the living room, we heard a knock. To my surprise, it was Evette. She asked to talk privately, so I politely excused myself and went downstairs to her apartment.

"Are you stupid?!" Evette asked as she shut the door. "You move in with those girls upstairs from me? That's mad disrespectful," she said with her East Coast accent.

"You broke up with me, remember? It shouldn't matter what I do. Where's your baby daddy anyway?" I responded sarcastically.

"Dre, don't do that. Honestly, since you left, I've realized what I lost and what I'd get back if I chose him. He didn't make parole, but even when he does, I don't want to go back to that lifestyle. I really love you, and I want to be with you. I'm sorry if I hurt you, but please move back in," she said as she started kissing my neck.

Everything inside told me not to be stupid, but I didn't care. If I were being honest, I missed her too. I loved Evette tremendously and appreciated what she did for me. Her judgments may have been off some, but she's human, right? After we made up, she made me go get my stuff from Tam's apartment. I've faced a lot of things in my life, but this was by far the hardest because I had sex with Tam the night before.

"Aye, I got something to tell y'all."

"Yo dumb ass is moving back in, ain't you?" Zion cut me off.

"Bro, it's not like that," I said, defending my decision.

"You ain't got to lie to me. How are you still in love with that bitch after what she did to you?" Zion snapped. "Let me guess, her baby daddy didn't make parole? You got this good woman right here and yet you go back to Evette?" I hadn't seen him this mad at me since the Kentucky trip.

"I love her, plus she apologized for that! Look, I'm not asking for your approval; I was just telling you to see if you were coming."

"Hell no, I'm staying here! That is… if it's ok with you Tam?" Zion asked.

"Of course," Tam said. She was visibly upset, but I wasn't expecting her to then turn to me and ask, "why Dre?"

My heart broke at the sight of Tam hurting because of my doing. I hurried to pack my belongings, trying to hold onto my emotions.

"If you really move back in with Evette, I swear bro I'm going to be mad. I can't even lie. Like don't fuck with me no more type of shit!" Zion warned.

I looked at Zion, and my heart dropped. I didn't know what to say, so I just stared at him.

"Matter of fact, just go!"

After he slammed the door in my face, I made my way back to Evette's, instantly regretting my decision. Zion has been a loyal friend who chose to be there no matter what. Is she really worth losing his friendship? And what about Tam? How can you hurt her when you don't even know if you can truly trust Evette anymore? My stomach knotted, and my head spun. I put my stuff down and went into the bedroom. I lay across the bed next to Evette and forced myself to fall asleep.

Later that night, I had the strangest dream that felt so real. Zion and I were laughing outside when a bunch of guys rolled up and started some beef. One minute we were fighting, and the next they killed him. I woke up, drenched in sweat. My face was moist because I had obviously been crying in my sleep. I looked over at the clock and noticed it was 3:00 a.m. Forcing myself to get out of bed, I made my way to the bathroom and removed my sweaty clothes. After turning the shower to the hottest setting, I got in and slumped under the water—staring off into deep thought.

Why did that dream feel so real? Is that God's way of telling me to make amends with Zion before it's too late? I closed my eyes and let the water trickle down my face as it rushed to my feet. After a few minutes, I decided to go approach Zion—thinking he should've calmed down by now. We have been through way worse, so there's no reason we can't work this out, I thought.

I began to feel myself panicking as my memory sank deeper into my internal wound.

Suddenly, I was distracted by the sound of Mrs. Karolyn reciting Isaiah 41:10, "Fear not, for I am with you; Be not dismayed, for I am your God. I will strengthen you, yes, I will help you. I will uphold you with My righteous right hand."

With nothing left to lose, I allowed myself to finally go to that space. As I drifted deeper into my memories, the darkness slowly engulfed the light.

## *10. Lost in the shuffle*

*"The Lord is close to the brokenhearted and saves those who are crushed in spirit."*

**—Psalm 34:18—**

The next morning, I set out to make amends with Zion. Luckily, I didn't have to go far because he was smoking a Newport on the stairs. We hadn't smoked marijuana since the beginning of our probation, but desperate times called for desperate measures. I knew we had at least 3 weeks before our next scheduled drug test, so I decided to roll a blunt as a peace offering. I hoped he wouldn't be able to resist, but looking back, I see that was the wrong call on my part.

"Don't fuck with me anymore," Zion's voice echoed in my head. Shaking it off, I approached him as I sparked the blunt. I hit it a few times, then passed it to him to see if he would accept it. He stared at me for a good minute, then smiled and grabbed the blunt.

"I can't lie, you pissed me off, but I will never turn my back on you. You should know that by now, especially after the bullshit you did in Kentucky. I almost beat your ass for that, but this is nowhere near the same. We're brothers, and brothers fight, but I'm sorry, fam," Zion said before hitting the blunt.

"Nah, bro, I'm sorry! You know I don't make the best decisions, especially when it pertains to females, but I never want that to interfere with our friendship," I said.

"Look, if you love Evette, that's your prerogative. I just think you deserve better. Part of being a friend is keeping it real with each other, but I will never let a female come between our brotherhood," Zion said.

I felt relieved hearing him say that, but I knew I still needed to tell him about my dream. I opened my mouth, but the words wouldn't come out.

"You good?" Zion asked, noticing something was off.

"Honestly, no," I said, trying to find the words. "I had a dream last night, and you died. I woke up crying because it felt so real. I don't know what I'd do if that actually happened. We've seen so many people pass away, and we never got the chance to say goodbye. God forbid anything were to happen to you, I want you to know that I love you and I really appreciate how you've been here for me during the hardest times of my life."

Zion looked at me as he hit the blunt a few more times and then passed it back. He released the built-up smoke and let a tear drop. This was the first time in my life I had ever seen Zion cry. After a moment of silence, he finally said, "Let's get baptized today."

"You serious?" I was shocked.

"Yeah, I've been thinking about it for a while now. I'm ready to change and give my life to God. I believe your dream was the confirmation I needed for my fresh start," Zion said confidently.

"Okay, let's do it then," I said, encouraged.

We went to my mother's church and shocked everyone with our baptism request. My mother was overwhelmed with joy as she watched us make a life-changing decision. We vowed to complete not only our 10-year probation but also college and become successful. After church, we drove back to the apartment complex and went our separate ways. I headed to Evette's, and he went upstairs to Tam's.

When I walked in, Evette was packing things into boxes. "Are we moving?" I asked, making sure it was still a 'we'.

"Hell yeah! You think I'm gonna continue living in the same building with the chick you were just smashing? Hell no! We are moving in with my mother until we can find a new apartment. Now go make yourself useful and get those chairs on the patio and load them up," Evette ordered.

When I opened the sliding door, I instantly smelled a foul odor. I looked down and saw flies and maggots gorging on what looked like raw chicken. I looked closer and saw they were all in the same spot, as if they'd been dropped from above, which meant only one thing. I know you're lying! First, they steal our stuff, and now they drop raw chicken on my girl's patio. They must not know who they're fucking with? I thought as I grabbed my phone and called Zion.

"Man, I'm about to go slide these niggas!" I yelled into the receiver.

"Who?!" Zion asked.

"Jerome and Jerold! Just come outside," I told him. When he came downstairs, I filled him in on what happened.

"Bro, you really want to fight over chicken?" Zion asked. "We just got baptized! Is it really worth it?"

Zion's words sparked a tingle in me, as if the Holy Spirit were trying to warn me, but I ignored it, refusing to look like a punk.

"Hell yeah," I confirmed, finally making up my mind.

"Aight, fine, but before we do this, I gotta go take a shit."

When Zion left, I went inside to put on my fighting shoes. Moments later, I walked out with Evette trailing me like I was on my way to a boxing ring. Ironically, when Zion finally came out, Tam was trailing him too.

"Dre, don't do this!" Tam said, trying to prevent a fight. "I threw that chicken."

"What kind of chicken was it, Tam?" I asked.

"Fried chicken! My bad, Dre, damn! But all this over chicken?" Tam said, once again trying to stop me.

"Nope, nice try! It was raw, and there were maggots and shit." I informed her.

"Boo, do you want me to go clean it up? It can't be that serious," Tam said.

"BOO?!" Evette chimed in. "Matter of fact, yes, bitch, come clean this up."

"Bitch? I will drag you!" Tam told Evette.

"Man, y'all chill with all that. I'm about to go check them," I told Evette and Tam.

"Dre, just think about it. You're about to fight over chicken," Tam tried to talk some sense into me.

"Bae, fuck that bitch. Go drop them niggas," Evette ordered.

Zion just stood there smiling but didn't say anything. I walked upstairs and started banging on Jerome and Jerold's door. When Jerold finally opened it, he reached out to shake my hand.

"Nah, which one of you dropped raw chicken on my patio?"

"Raw chicken? Why would we do that? We're grown men; we would've thrown the chicken away," Jerold said condescendingly.

"Forget that, bae. Don't listen to his ass. Drop him!" Evette shouted.

"It's crazy you say that, but how do you explain multiple pieces plopped directly under your balcony?" I interrogated.

"HEY! You all need to move around. If you don't live here, then you need to leave the premises," the apartment security officer said, overhearing all the commotion.

"Yeah! Y'all move around," Jerome said as he walked up behind Jerold, trying to sound tough.

"You think you're safe because the Rent-a-cop is here? I'll still drop you," I said before the security guard stepped in between us. "It's cool, we'll be back," I said.

Zion and I hopped in my car and left the complex. We drove away from the scene to let things die down, only to return thirty minutes later, hungry for blood. I marched back up to their apartment and started pounding on their door again.

"Wassup now!" I yelled.

When they opened the door, I was surprised to see another person with them. Unfazed by being outnumbered, Zion said, "Bring y'all ass downstairs so nobody gets thrown over."

He and I walked down the stairs first, with Jerome, Jerold, and the random guy following.

"This is what y'all want? Over some raw chicken?" the random asked.

"Man, we're done talking," I said, once again letting my ego rule me.

Everything happened so quickly. Zion threw a two-piece and connected on both hits. The random took a few steps back to gather himself, then quickly countered Zion with two of his own. Zion weaved one, but the second connected, hitting him in the eye.

"Ahhh!" Zion screamed as he backed away.

I rushed the random. I jumped through the air—landing a right hook to his face. He grabbed hold of my shirt and pulled me down, causing us to tumble downhill. Luckily for him, he landed on top of me. I guarded my face as he started swinging. Catching onto one of his arms, I used every bit of strength I had to roll him over—allowing me to flip on top of him. I hammered into his face until I felt someone trying to grab me off.

"STOP!! STOP!!" Tam pleaded.

I pushed her off me and went back to punching my target. Tam got up and tried again.

"DRE! STOP! Please!!!" Tam begged. "THEY STABBED ZION!"

Tam's words temporarily froze time, and all I could hear was the sound of my heart beating. My eyes slowly scanned the area until they locked onto Zion. I could feel the overextension of my eyelids as I watched him stumble, clutching his chest. I instantly went into shock, and my body was paralyzed. Tears began to form in my eyes as I stood there watching his white T-shirt slowly become saturated with the red of his blood.

I felt an urge for revenge. I reached for my strap, but then I remembered I didn't have it. Zion didn't want us to bring any weapons in case things went bad, so we wouldn't be tempted to use them.

"You ok, bro?" I asked Zion.

"Get me to a hospital," Zion said as he collapsed onto me. I flung his arm over my shoulder and started dragging him to my car.

"Who did this?"

"Jerome!" Zion answered, coughing up blood.

At this point, I was supporting all of Zion's body weight. As we approached my car, I opened the door and tried to help Zion in, but he slid down—no longer able to stand. I tried to lift him again, but before I could close the door, we were ambushed by 10 police officers with their guns drawn.

"GET ON THE GROUND!" one officer yelled.

"He's been stabbed!" I yelled back. Then, out of nowhere, another officer slammed me to the ground and cuffed me. He sat me on the stairs as I watched the other officers apply pressure to Zion's wounded chest. I didn't know what was going to happen. I wanted to save Zion, but I couldn't. All I could do was watch my best friend suffer while we waited for the EMTs to arrive. Feeling useless, I nearly went crazy when I saw two officers escorting Jerome and Jerold in cuffs to a squad car.

"Ima kill y'all! I swear to God!" I screamed as the cop nearby restrained me. When I noticed no other officers were following them, I yelled, "Where is the third guy?"

"What third guy?" the officer asked.

"There were three people. Not two," I informed him. Another officer went back to the apartment only to return empty-handed.

He must've run away with the knife, and these stupid motherfuckers let him, I thought. My Superman was down, and there was nothing I could do. What made matters worse was that when the EMTs finally arrived, nobody knew the damn gate code to let them through.

"Zion? Are you okay? Say something," I begged.

"DRE! I can't breathe…" Zion cried

Tam dropped to his side and grabbed his hand. I could hear her telling him to fight as she tried to comfort him.

"Tam, tell my mama I love her, and I'm sorry," Zion wept.

I couldn't breathe; I wanted to trade places so badly. If I hadn't switched fighters, I would be lying there, not him. Why the hell didn't I listen? I thought, angry with myself. Suddenly, an elderly lady from the neighborhood walked up and grabbed Zion's hand, asking him if he believed in Jesus Christ.

"Yes," Zion confessed.

"Then pray with me," she said, and she prayed over Zion.

Please, Lord, save him. I promise I'll clean up my act and live a Godly life. Please don't take Zion away from me. I tried bargaining with God.

I resisted arrest as the officer tried to stand me up and put me in the back of his squad car. I did everything I could to stay with my friend a little longer. He needed me, and I needed him. Despite my attempts, I was not strong enough to break free. I was thrown into the back of the car with the door slammed shut. I looked up and saw them putting Evette and Tam into another police car together. Not allowing my mind to wander about what they were talking about, I shifted my focus back to Zion.

Watching as the EMTs put him on a stretcher, I screamed, "ZION!" I started kicking the back window and crying as the squad car pulled away. All I wanted to do was be there for Zion the same way he had always been there for me.

The police drove to the station and threw me into one of those rooms you see on First 48. Pacing back and forth, my mind was running wild until two detectives finally came in and started to question me. I demanded that they tell me Zion's status before I answered any of their questions. When they told me he was in critical condition, I was willing to cooperate with them. I knew the only way to get justice was to be 100% honest, so I told them everything. I even admitted that I started the fight. I poured my heart out about how much Zion meant to me, and I could tell they believed me. In fact, one officer even said so. The problem was that without the weapon or an admission of guilt, they couldn't do anything. They also mentioned inconsistencies between Tam and Evette's stories, and of course, Jerome and Jerold weren't saying anything to clarify. The officers told me to hang tight before they left me there to suffer with my overthinking mind.

I fell on my knees and prayed. "Jesus, please save Zion. Please! You said, "Ask, and I shall receive." I'm not asking, Lord; I am begging at Your throne. Heal him and keep him alive. I can't live without my brother, Lord," I said aloud before curling up and crying myself to sleep. Hours flew by before I woke up. Realizing this wasn't just a terrible nightmare, my mind drifted back to Zion. I jumped up and banged on the door, demanding answers. I kicked and screamed until, eventually, an officer came.

"Follow me," was all he said as he led me into an office. When we walked in, three other officers were waiting near the telephone. They all stared at me as if they were studying my body language. I sat down as instructed and noticed the desk clock read 5:27 am.

"There's someone on the phone who wants to talk to you. But…before we give it to you, you need to promise you'll control yourself," the officer began.

I simply nodded my head in agreement as I picked up the receiver. "Hello?... Zion?"

"Baby…" My mother said in a tone that caused my whole body to go numb. "Zion didn't make it…" Everything else she said instantly muted. I had sunk into a dark space, only to be revived by the news that he had passed away at 9 pm the night before. My insides were set ablaze as I blacked out—attacking everyone in my sight. When they were finally able to restrain me, I gave up and cried uncontrollably in an officer's arms. Suddenly, the memory of Tam trying to prevent the fight sucker punched me; I went limp, having no more strength to live.

. . .

"You see, Mrs. Karolyn? It's all my fault! I just couldn't walk away. I had to prove a point, and look what happened!"

"Oh, Dre!" Mrs. Karolyn said as she got up from her chair and walked around to hug me. "I understand now! I know it doesn't feel good to hear this, but you were blessed with a second chance at life. Do you honestly think Zion would want you to spend the rest of it in pain? What about God?" She squeezed me tighter before releasing me from her embrace. "Dre, God does everything for a reason. Isaiah 55:8 says, 'For my thoughts are not your thoughts, neither are your ways my ways.' We don't know the reasoning behind God's plan; we are only to trust Him. Maybe He called Zion home because he was at the peak of his walk. Maybe this was the only way to get your attention."

"Why?" I cried, confused.

"I'm not entirely sure, but that's why you need to open your Bible. One reason I recite Scripture is because I believe in its power. Faith comes from hearing, and hearing the word of God. During my darkest times, it was the Scriptures that saved me and kept me going. God blessed me after my turmoil, and now He's using me for His glory. No matter how the devil tries to deceive you, stay encouraged because God will make everything right. If He did it for Daniel and me, He'll do it for you," Mrs. Karolyn said, trying to continue before I interrupted.

"How? If I had just listened to everyone, Zion would still be here, and his family wouldn't be hurting. What makes it worse is that someone started a rumor that I left Zion stranded to die. Can you believe that? People I once trusted have turned their backs on me; they even think it's my fault. I swear I didn't mean for him to die! I tried to help him. I fought with all my heart. Since Zion isn't here to defend me, I have to live with guilt and lies. When I find

126

out who started that rumor, I promise I will show them how hard I fought," I swore.

"Dre, that is not the answer. Haven't you learned by now that violence only brings more chaos? Listen, we are going to stop here for today, but I want you to spend tonight doing two homework assignments. After hearing what happened to Zion, it dawned on me that perhaps one of the reasons you're struggling is that you weren't there when he passed away. I know you never got the chance to say goodbye, so tonight I want you to write Zion a letter. Whatever is in your heart, let yourself release it onto the page. Secondly, and this is important, you must learn to control your anger. I have heard about multiple incidents where you acted on impulse, which is probably how you got those five counts of aggravated assault. Go home, think about your future, and imagine where your life will be in the next five years," Mrs. Karolyn instructed.

"What I want doesn't even matter, because I'll still be on probation. We were supposed to finish this together, and now I have to do all these years by myself. You might as well just send me to prison. I can't take this anymore," I said, defeated.

"Father God, I come to You now and beg You to heal Dre's broken heart. Give him the strength to endure, even when his mind cannot comprehend Your reasoning. Transform his pain into triumph so that he may use his testimony to help others. Thank You for sending Your son, Jesus, to die for our sins, so Zion, my niece, Dre, and I have the chance to enter Your Heavenly Kingdom. Replace his guilt and shame with Your joy and peace, Lord. I ask all of this in Your Holy name. Amen," Ms. Karolyn closed, looking lovingly into my eyes.

Her prayer somehow soothed the hurt that had built up within. For the first time in a while, I felt understood and accepted. "Thank you, Mrs. Karolyn. I will never forget you and all that you've done to help me. Please don't stop believing in me! I may not love nor forgive myself right now, but you give me so much hope," I admitted.

"Well, thank you, Dre. I am positive I will never forget you either," she smiled and hugged me again. "Remember, give it to God. Stop holding all that guilt in; forgive yourself. Once you do that, you'll start to see a shift," Mrs. Karolyn promised.

"Yes, ma'am, I'll try," I lied.

Forgiving myself was not an option! I will forever hold this against me and take accountability for the death of my best friend, I thought as I walked to my car. When I hopped in, I sat there in silence before I could face it. I looked over to the passenger's side door and started sobbing. The last thing I had to remember Zion—was the old smudge of his blood that would forever ride around with me.

## *11. The Seed:*

*"I ask you not to lose heart at my tribulations for you, which is your glory."*
**—Ephesians 3:13 (NIV) –**

Today marked the anniversary of Zion's death, and all I wanted to do was wake up from this horrific nightmare. Since Tam and I hadn't made up yet, I decided to go to my car to wake in bake in peace. I reached into the glove compartment and retrieved my old phone. I sparked my blunt and scrolled through the only pictures I had left of us. I then played my favorite video of Zion clowning me because he beat me in Madden. When I heard his loud, obnoxious laugh, I instantly broke down. Every day, I wish I could go back to that night. I would just walk away like you wanted, I thought. I put the car in reverse and turned on the radio. Ironically, Lil Wayne's "I Miss My Dawgs" was playing, which ignited the fuse o my guilt. When I exited the apartment complex, I floored it. With tears rushing down my face, I continued to pick up speed with no intention of slowing down.

Fuck my life! I can't take this anymore. I should just kill myself! The voices from the past started playing in my head, telling me it should have been me instead; telling me that I am not a good friend since I haven't gotten revenge; telling me that I didn't fight hard enough or that I didn't at all. Then there were echoes of the other voices saying, "It's been months, get over it, man the fuck up, stop being a victim," and making it about me. Yet the loudest of them all yelled, "You're the reason Zion is dead."

"I CAN'T TAKE THIS ANYMORE!" I screamed out loud, triggered by the antagonizing memories. Everything in me told me to crash into the oncoming traffic. Convinced this route would solve everything, I accelerated and started to say my last goodbyes. As I went through the names of my loved ones, I visualized their faces until an image of Dre Dre standing over my casket, crying, flashed before my eyes. I slammed on my brakes, and when the car finally stopped skidding, I sat there sobbing in the center of the intersection. Knowing the pain Zion's family endured, I couldn't bear the thought of inflicting the same pain on my own, especially not on Dre Dre.

BBBBEEEEEEEEPPPPPPPP! The car behind me honked at me to move. Numb to what I almost did, I drove in silence to my appointment with Mrs. Karolyn. When I got there, I broke down in her arms and told her what had just happened.

"SIT! NOW!" she demanded.

I did as I was told, sitting down in the black cushioned seat. I really wasn't trying to hear it today. *As a matter of fact, it's all her fault for picking at my wound.*

"So, your answer to all of this is to kill yourself? What is that going to solve, Dre? What about your kids?" Mrs. Karolyn asked.

"You don't understand how this eats me up inside every single day. People tell me it's not my fault, but I don't see it that way. Zion's family is hurting because of me, and I know for a fact that if I hadn't started the fight, he would still be here. Now I am stuck with his blood on my hands," I cried. "What makes things worse is that the cops didn't even charge them with murder. So, his mother will never get closure, nor will he get the justice he deserves!"

"I'm confused. Jerome and Jerold aren't in jail?" Mrs. Karolyn asked.

"You would think so, but this is America. A couple of weeks after Zion was killed, two detectives came to my mother's house and asked to speak privately in their squad car. They informed me that without a weapon, confession, or any concrete evidence, they would have to rule his death as an accident. Then they mentioned some B.S about it being an election year, as if Zion wasn't important enough to keep the case open. Can you believe that? They got away with murder, and the only thing I can do is seek revenge or live with the guilt for the rest of my life."

"First of all, 'vengeance is mine, says the Lord!' That is not for you to dish out, because that will only land you in prison, and then who will raise your kids? I am sorry they weren't charged, and I am sorry about how this has impacted you, but killing yourself will not fix any of that. I know it can be overbearing at times, but you must fight through it and just get to the next day. Did you write the letter to Zion as I instructed?" Mrs. Karolyn asked.

"No, and honestly, I don't feel like talking about it anymore. Ever since I started talking with you, the pain feels worse than it did when it was fresh."

"Dre, my job is to find the root of the problem so that we can begin your healing. I never said the pain would instantly go away. It's going to require a lot of hard work and self-discipline. Speaking of which, I can smell that you're still smoking. You need to stop that before you wind up in prison," Mrs. Karolyn scolded. "I know you think smoking helps, but it's only a temporary fix. Once the high comes down, the pain is still there, so is it really helping?"

"Would you rather have me smoke or commit suicide? That temporary high, as you call it, calms me down just enough to keep from doing the extreme. So yes, I would say it does help."

"Dre, you were fortunate enough to get 10 years of Deferred Adjudication Probation. All you have to do is follow the orders, finish these next 9 years, and it'll be off your record. Or you can spend that time in prison; it's up to you."

"I have been smoking since I was thirteen years old," I confessed. "It's the only thing I know that helps take away the pain."

"You smoke to avoid dealing with the pain, but guess what, in a few hours it'll resurface. Then you're going to smoke again, only this time the high lasts shorter because of your tolerance. Do you see where I am going? You can't put a band-aid on a deep wound," Mrs. Karolyn said.

"Maybe so, but every day I feel like dying! I wake up to the realization that Zion is never coming back, and it's all my fault. He wasn't the one who should have died that day; it should have been me. Now everyone hates and blames me, so why not just end my life here? It's not like anyone would care anyway."

"Your family would care, more importantly, your sons need you, Dre! Think about what would happen if you weren't in their lives. Do you want a man like Manny raising them? Suicide may seem like a pain-free option, but you're not thinking about the magnitude of your actions. Your family would still feel the burden. What you've been through at such a young age was for a reason. Going through all those experiences will help you get through any future adversity. Ephesians 3:13 says, 'Therefore I ask that you do not lose heart at my tribulations for you, which is your glory.' God wants you to trust Him because He trusts you. He knows that this is hard, but He also knows there is something in you that can pass this test and transform the lives of others through your affliction. It's not just about Zion, your sons, or even you; it's for everyone who looks like you and comes from where you come from, to witness what God can do. You never know, Dre! Your story could have an influential impact on the community, but if you're not alive to tell it, then you'll be like all the other great stories that were buried in the grave," Mrs. Karolyn said. "Now let's get back to work because when it comes to the Lord, I can talk all day," Mrs. Karolyn then let out a scream of joy.

"You sound like my mom," I chuckled.

"Well, your mother must be a fine woman of God. Speaking of your mother, you mentioned she was the one who informed you that Zion passed, correct?" Mrs. Karolyn questioned, getting us back on track.

"Yes, ma'am."

"How did she find out? And who told Zion's mother?" Mrs. Karolyn asked.

"My little sister and Dre Dre were at the apartment, helping Evette and I move, so she told my mother. Then my mother called Zion's mom and informed her. While all that was going on, the cops kept me overnight in the homicide unit to give Jerome and Jerold enough time to quickly vacate their apartment. When I was finally released, I was escorted to my mother's house, where my siblings were waiting for me. It was a bittersweet reunion, but I was grateful they were all there for me. After that, I went to Zion's mother's house to give her my condolences. His entire family was there and wanted to know what happened. I will never forget the look on their faces, nor how Zion's mother almost fainted when I told them Zion died over raw chicken. Everyone was so disappointed. The reality that he wasn't coming back finally sank in as the pain rushed into every cavity of my heart. In that moment, I wished I could trade places with him. To this day, I still don't understand why God kept me here when Zion could have been something in this life," I confessed.

"Dre, God doesn't make mistakes. You must take back the power over your life so you can become the man God is calling you to be. Imagine yourself sitting in the driver's seat. You have two side mirrors and one rearview mirror, which are designed to help prevent you from crashing while switching lanes. Those mirrors are your past. Next, you have your windshield, intentionally made larger so you're focused on where God is sending you. Much like life, your past can help you navigate through hard times, but if you stay focused on it for too long, you'll eventually crash. However, by using those memories as intended—to reference and help you move forward—you'll reach your destination much safer. Finally, you have your steering wheel, and you know whose hands are on it, Dre?"

"Mine," I answered, understanding her analogy.

"Correct! Your hands, meaning you're controlling your destination. We are taught to keep our eyes on the road (Jesus) to avoid objects. Have you ever seen a deer run out in front of you while you were driving?"

"This is Texas, of course," I admitted.

"Problems in life are like those deer that just jump out of nowhere. Take control of your life and yield to the oncoming trials and tribulations. Stay focused on your future and what lies ahead. Don't allow your past to send you to an early grave. Instead, let it help guide you to where you want to go in life," Mrs. Karolyn said. "Now, I see that today is the anniversary of Zion's death. I need you to be strong and not smoke! They are looking for a reason to lock you up, so promise me!"

"I promise," I lied.

"Dre, please keep your promise, because I'd hate to see you go to prison. That would really break my heart," Mrs. Karolyn said firmly. "Well, that is all for today. I will see you Monday morning, correct?"

"Yes, ma'am," I guaranteed.

"Have a good weekend, but be mindful that you have a meeting with your probation officer next week as well. He'll be requesting my notes, but if you fail your drug test, there's nothing I can say or do to save you," Mrs. Karolyn reminded me.

"Yes, ma'am," I hugged her before I left her office.

While I was driving, I began to smell the weed I had in my secret stash. As tempted as I was, I looked at my hands on the wheel, and Mrs. Karolyn's words registered. I cracked my window, letting the fresh air force its way inside. I grabbed my stash and threw everything out. For some reason, I began to feel a little bit of hope trying to shine its way through the darkness of my soul. I made up my mind that I would stop smoking and do right, but first, I needed to make amends with Tam.

As soon as I opened the door, she was there waiting to talk, but I cut her off.

"Tam, I know it doesn't change how you feel, but I want you to know that I am sorry for disrespecting you and calling you out of your name. I am also sorry for destroying our home once again. I know you just want peace, but I have so much going on in my mind. Still, the last thing I want to do is lose …"

"I'm pregnant," Tam said, interrupting me.

"What? Are you serious!?" I asked, excited.

"Yes!" Tam confirmed. "But look at me, Dre. You must forgive yourself. It's not your fault that Zion died! I know that saying you should have listened to me and maybe he'd still be alive was wrong and probably adds to what eats you up, but I can't take it back; no matter how much I wish I could. I am truly sorry from the bottom of my heart. I want you to get better not only for you but for our child," she said, rubbing her belly.

"I forgive you, but you were right. I don't want you to feel guilty for telling me what was real—if I had listened to you, Zion wouldn't have died. Still, I will work on improving myself, especially for my daughter, but I will NEVER forgive myself!" I said, trying to change the subject.

"First, you don't know if it's a girl, and second, you can't get better without forgiving yourself, Dre!" Tam assured.

"Honestly, Tam, if forgiving myself is part of healing, I guess I'll never be fully healed."

"I really hate it when you talk like that. Is Mrs. Karolyn helping at all?"

"No matter what anybody says, Zion's blood is on my hands! You can't help me, my mother can't help me, Mrs. Karolyn can't help me, Pastor can't help me, NOBODY CAN HELP ME! Because I know that if I didn't start that fight, Zion would still be alive!"

Tam didn't speak. Instead, she stared at me with teary, concerned eyes.

"Exactly!" I answered for her.

She came over and hugged me as I broke down in her arms. All I could think about was OCTOBER 11TH! One year feels like a day to me. I'm so sorry, Zion. I swear to God I wish I could go back and stop the fight, bro. I wish I could do something to make this right.

I cried harder into Tam's arm as my mind raced at 1000 mph. I cried for a few minutes until my security wall came back up. "I need to smoke," I said as I wiped away my tears.

"You know you can't smoke! Mrs. Karolyn called and told me that if you fail one more drug test, they will send you to prison. You don't want to miss out on our child's birth, do you?" Tam asked, hoping her words would get through to me this time.

"You're right, Tam! Today is the day I stop smoking, for our daughter," I said, speaking it into existence.

"Yeah, okay, don't be disappointed when it's a boy," Tam joked.

I laid across the couch, drained from all the crying I had done today. Our son, Zion, must have felt the same because he crawled to me, whining. I picked Zion up and snuggled with him as we both fell sound asleep.

Suddenly, a loud knock at the door woke me up. I gently placed Zion in his pack-and-play before I went to the door. I checked the peephole, but it was covered. I figured it was my childish little brother, Toni.

"Who is it?" I said in my deep voice.

"Fort Worth Police Department, open up! We have a warrant for the arrest of Andre Shephard Jr."

## *12. Mercy*

*"Yea, though I walk through the valley of the shadow of death, I will fear no evil:
for thou art with me; thy rod and thy staff they comfort me."*
**—Psalm 23:4 (KJV) –**

"Dre!" Zion shouted in excitement. I couldn't believe my eyes;
all I could do was cry as I hugged him for dear life.

"Zion, I am so sorry! I should have listened to you!" I cried
out.

"It's okay, bro. I forgive you, but look at your life, fam. I can't
believe you are going to prison, just like your real dad and Manny.
Dre, this isn't the way for you! God has so much in store, but you
must trust in Him and let Him direct your path. I need you to know
that I am okay and in a far better place. Please forgive yourself and
give the pain to God." Zion was different, and the Holy Spirit in
me could feel it, too.

"Bro, just take me with you, please," I begged.

"I wish, but it's not your time! God has a calling on your life
and wants to use you! Use this pain and experience to help bring
others to God."

"I'm mad at God! Why didn't He answer my prayers and save
you as I asked?" I questioned.

"He did save me, and that's what you fail to understand! To be
absent from the flesh is to be present with the Lord! You may not
realize it now, but later you will understand! While you are
incarcerated, open your Bible and draw closer to God as He draws
closer to you!"

"CHOW TIME!" the guard yelled, waking me from my sleep.
"Sleep late, lose weight!" So that's where Zion got that from, I
thought.

Recalling my dream, I became furious because once again I
didn't get the chance to say goodbye. I hated that part about being
incarcerated: every time I woke up, I was snatched from the free

world only to be thrown back into the trenches of my new reality. This was my first time in the Green Bay Jail of Tarrant County, and it was truly hell on earth. Anyone who has ever stepped foot in there would agree. From the kennel-like cells, the mystery meat they called food, to the power-tripping guards, who were clearly bullied in school, my soul knew this would be my first and last time.

There were 32 bunk beds lined up in a row, and I absolutely hated being in a dorm with 63 other men. It stunk like armpits and ass. On top of that, egos were through the roof, like we were seniors in high school. The funniest part was that everybody was at the top of their crime class. If you were in there for selling drugs, you were like Scarface. If you were in there for gun charges, you were like Rambo. If you served in the military, you swore you were in the Navy Seals. That is how Jail became an acronym for **J**ust **A**sk **I**'ll **L**ie.

Oh, and let's not forget the repeat offenders who were everyone's personal incarcerated attorney. They've been locked up so many times that they will give you their expert testimony about your case and how to beat it. Many of them didn't have a clue what they were talking about, but a few did. Besides all of that, it's been two months since I last smoked, and that was punishment itself. This has been the longest I have ever gone without weed since I started smoking at 13 years old.

I hopped off the top bunk, immediately feeling a sharp pain in my back from the hard mattress I was forced to sleep on. I put on my green jumpsuit and got in line for my breakfast tray. Yet another thing I could never get used to about jail: the feeding hours. They served breakfast at 5:30 a.m., lunch at 11:30, and Dinner at 5:00 p.m. If you missed any of them and didn't have commissary, you were S.O.L. I was told to expect the same hours in prison, except better food and cheaper commissary. When I got my tray, I sold it to my homie J Dunn for two soups. I met him the very first time I ever got locked up.  A lot of people get out and say they are going to put money on your books or call someone for you and never do it, but J Dunn was one of the few solid ones who did. The funny thing was, every time I went to jail after that, guess who I saw? Only this time, both J Dunn and I were headed to prison.

I hardly ever ate breakfast, but even if I wanted to, I couldn't today. In just a few hours, I will be standing before a judge to receive my prison sentence. My stomach was literally in pain from fear and anxiety. Every "incarcerated attorney" I talked to told me I was facing a minimum of 10 years. I had reached out to my court-appointed attorney many times, but to no avail. All I could think about was missing the birth of my unborn child in Tam's stomach.

I went back to my bunk and pulled out my Bible. I didn't know where to begin, so I prayed and asked God to guide and speak to me. I randomly opened the Bible, and coincidentally, Ephesians 3:13 was highlighted by the previous owner.

"Therefore, I ask that you do not lose heart at my tribulations for you, which is your glory," I read out loud as goose bumps formed, remembering when Mrs. Karolyn first recited this to me. I finally understood the message. I fell to my knees, and I prayed for the first time since Zion's death.

*Dear Heavenly Father, I'm sorry it's been so long, but I've been so angry and hurt inside for some time now. I may never know why you didn't save Zion, but right now I need you to save me. I am scared and worried, because I cannot serve 10 years in prison, Lord. Last time I prayed, I asked to be set free, but now I just ask that you show me mercy in the sentencing. Please also protect Tam, my boys, and my unborn child. Lord, please let it be a girl. I pray for all of this in*

*Your Holy Name, Amen.*

Later that morning, I was escorted to the Tarrant County Courthouse by the correctional officers. The closer I got, the harder it was to breathe. I have seen a lot of movies and heard many horror stories about prison, so the less time I got, the better.

The officers put me in a holding cell while I waited for my court-appointed attorney. I didn't even know what he sounded like, let alone how he looked. I started pacing around in the small cell, "Lord, please do it for me!" I pleaded one last time before I was interrupted.

"Mr. Shephard? I am your attorney, Mr. Walker," the gentleman introduced himself with his thick country accent.

"Yes, sir, how are you?" I asked, unbothered by his lack of response over the past two months.

"I'm doing just fine, my friend. You, on the other hand, it's not looking so pretty," he said nonchalantly. "The District Attorney is offering you 10 years in prison. With the year of probation you completed, you'd only have to serve 9."

9 YEARS! My unborn will be 8, Dre Dre will be 14. I don't want to miss all that time with my children. Please, Lord, no!

"Look, sir, I'm going to be honest with you. I can't do 9 years in prison. Please tell the judge that my best friend was stabbed in front of me. I am sorry for violating my probation, but I've been emotionally broken ever since his death. I am not asking to be set free at all; I just ask that the judge be lenient with me. Can you ask for 2 years T.D.C?" I begged.

Mr. Walker laughed. "Sure, I'll go ask, but don't hold your breath. I highly doubt this D.A. is going to come down from the 10-year offer."

As my lawyer left, I fell to my knees once again.

Lord, please show me Your mercy. That's all I ask! I don't deserve it, but please open the windows of heaven and pour down a blessing. Please protect me during my sentence, for you said, As I walk through the valley of the shadow of death, I shall fear no evil, for You are with me. You promised to never leave me nor forsake me, so please continue to stand with me as I feel alone. I ask all this in Jesus' name! Amen.

Mr. Walker returned shortly after, accompanied by a correctional officer, and instructed me to follow him. I panicked as we walked through the courtroom doors, unsure of what I was about to face. I looked around and, to my surprise, saw Mrs. Karolyn sitting next to the D.A. I scanned the courtroom until I locked eyes with Tam. I wanted to run to her and hug her, but the shackles on my feet held me back. Next to her was my mother, sobbing. She was surely feeling hopeless and powerless, wanting to do anything to save her baby. It hurt me so much that I couldn't comfort Tam and my mother.

"Mr. Shephard," the judge called out.

"Yes, your honor?" I politely answered.

"I see that you signed for 10 years' probation and have completed only one year. However, in that year, you didn't pay your probation fees or finish the required classes. In addition, I see here that you have 13 dirty UAs." He paused as he took off his glasses. "13 failed drug tests? That is ridiculous, Mr. Shephard! I have sent offenders to prison for a lot less. It seems to me that you've been getting chance after chance. Why should I give you 2 years' T.D.C instead of making you serve the remainder of your time?"

"Your honor, I am not going to sit here and make up any excuses about the dirty UAs. It has been very hard dealing with the death of my best friend. The guilt I hold onto, the lack of justice he and his family received, and the fact that he's not coming back make every day a struggle for me. I was getting help from Mrs. Karolyn, but I understand my actions are why we are here today. Even though it has been a whole year, I am still healing. I am sorry I couldn't stop smoking sooner, but that was the only thing keeping me alive. I have made a lot of bad decisions, like the fight

I started that got my best friend killed. His blood is on my hands, and smoking was the only thing that helped ease the pain. I attempted suicide a couple of times, but couldn't leave my kids. I know I deserve to go to prison, but all that I ask is that you don't send me away for a long time; that'll only institutionalize me and make my mental health worse. I also have a pregnant wife and other children who need me. All I ask is for mercy," I begged.

"You know what, Mr. Shephard? In my 30 years of experience, I have never had a case like this. I had a long conversation with Mrs. Karolyn, who I understand has been advocating on your behalf. She begged that I show mercy on you as well and send you to a facility where you would receive help. While I do see you have completed some of the requirements, it's these 13 dirty UA's I can't look past. Now you are aware I have the power to send you away for the remainder of your probation," the judge paused as he thought about my verdict.

"Yes, sir, your honor," my stomach sank lower as sweat began to pour from my pores.

"Mr. Shephard, I am going to sentence you to 3 years at the Texas Department of Corrections, and I will also make sure that you receive the counseling you need. You have my sincerest condolences for the loss of your friend, Zion Blake, but let this be a lesson that every decision you make from here on out will impact your future either positively or negatively. Hopefully, I will not see you back in my courtroom."

"Thank you, your honor," I said, grateful for the reduced sentence. "May I hug my mother one last time?"

"Yes, you may," the judge granted.

I hugged my mother and Tam tightly, knowing this would be our last embrace for a while. We said our goodbyes as the officer ushered me out of the courtroom. Before we reached the exit, Mrs. Karolyn approached and gave me a big hug, as tears streamed down her face.

"Mrs. Karolyn, thank you for keeping your promise not to give up on me. I am sorry I let you down, but I appreciate everything you did to help me. Therefore, I ask that you do not lose heart at my tribulations for you, which is your glory," I quoted from memory.

"That's right, son! Continue to read and study God's word; He'll protect you. Keep seeking him, and please stay encouraged, Dre," Mrs. Karolyn said as she released me.

"I will," I assured her as the officer escorted me away.

As soon as I made it back to my cell, the officer informed me that I had a visitor. When I reached the visitation area, I saw my mother sitting, still crying. My heart yearned for her; all I wanted to do was hold her, but we were separated by the glass.

"You got 30 minutes," the officer said after shutting the visitation door behind me.

"You okay?" I asked as a tear fell from my cheek.

"No," my mother answered honestly. "Are you okay?"

"No, but I will be. I was blessed, Mama; I prayed as you taught me, and God answered my prayers."

"What did you pray for? Mine didn't get answered," she said, sobbing.

"I prayed for mercy! 3 years is Him doing just that. Do you know they first offered 9 years, but I asked for 2, and my attorney laughed in my face? He even said he doubted the DA would come down from the offer," I told her. My mother's eyes widened.

"Wow, are you serious? I guess that is a blessing, because if 3 years hurts this bad, I could only imagine how I'd feel if I heard 9 years. I just wish I could be in there with you…" she said as she got up, unable to contain her emotions any longer.

Tam then sat down, and all I could do was notice the growth of her baby bump.

"Hey, baby," she said. "How are you doing in there?"

"I'm good, thanks for putting that money on my books. I've just been staying out of the way and working out. What about you and the baby? Where's Zion? Did you find out what we're having?" I had so many questions I couldn't ask them fast enough.

"We're all doing well. Zion is at home with your sister; he can talk now and misses you a lot! He walks around saying Da Da like he's looking for you; it's so cute. I paid the rent and utilities in advance with your check, so we'd be okay."

"That was smart," I said, feeling good that I was still able to provide for my family with my S.S.I. check.

"Okay! I was going to put this in a letter, but since you asked, I have some good news!" She paused dramatically. "It's a girl!" she screamed excitedly.

I was speechless; I just stared lovingly at her stomach. I put my head down in shame as the reality of not being present at my first daughter's birth tormented me.

"I'll never forgive myself for missing your birthday, Ana'Kele!" I cried out as my soul crumbled.

"Ana'Kele?" Tam asked, confused.

"It means Andre in Hawaiian. My grandma Ann told me that as a child, and I always wanted to name my daughter that," I told her.

"Dre, that's beautiful. Ana'Kele," Tam said, letting the name flow. "Yes! We'll name her Ana'Kele Christian Faith Shephard, meaning Andre, you're a Christian, so have Faith because your God's Shephard. Use our daughter's name to help you stay focused on God, and when times get hard, just remember the message."

"Wow," I said, moved by the deep message from my wife's heart.

"Time's up, Mr. Shephard!" Officer Wheeler said in what felt like the fastest 30 minutes of my life.

"Let our daughter be your motivation and stay on the right track. I'll be here every step of the way, waiting for you to return home. I love you," Tam said as she got up to leave.

"I love you, too," I responded.

Now, I was told it usually takes 30 days from the day you're sentenced to "catch chain" or be shipped to your assigned unit. I was happy because Christmas was the following week, and I figured I'd get to see my family before heading to prison. However, to my surprise, I was instructed to pack up because the transfer was going to happen that night. According to every "incarcerated attorney," this was the fastest they'd ever seen someone catch a chain, which only put more fear into my heart because I didn't get the chance to mentally prepare.

*Lord, as I walk through the valley of the shadow of death, I will fear no evil: for thou art with me; thy rod and thy staff they comfort me.* I quoted in my head as I sat on the white bus with tiny holes, which only allowed a glimpse of the free world. I was told I was heading to what the inmates called, Butt Naked Gurney. I had no clue how the unit got a name like that, but I didn't want any parts.

When we finally arrived, I saw a massive white facility with barbed wire fences surrounding the premises. As we entered, the gate to freedom closed behind us. When the bus came to a complete stop, the guards waiting escorted us off and made us form a line.

"Line up NOW! Face forward, NUTS TO ASS!" The one with Sergeant stripes ordered.

*Nuts to ass? Where the hell did the Judge send me?* I thought as I turned to warn the person behind me not to get too close.

"I see we have some new fish", the Sgt. said, noticing my reaction. "Welcome, to the sharks, welcome back. Let's get one thing clear, I am Sgt. Wallace, not B.O.S.S, Stupid Son of a…you know the rest. I run the show here. If you don't like it, don't bring your ass back. Now, listen up because I am only going to say this once! I don't give a rat's ass what you did to bring your ugly asses here, but while you are on this unit, you will abide by the rules, or your ass is grass. You get three strikes, and you're out. Meaning, I will G4 your ass quicker than a heartbeat if you violate the rules here. If you're new and don't know what G4 is or the rules here at Gurney, I advise you to study the Prison Handbook. Now, if you have been here before, you know how we get down and what time it is! Strip all your clothes off and line up nuts to ass." Sgt. Wallace ordered once again.

"Get naked and line nuts to ass?" I questioned, not believing my ears.

"Yes, do you have a problem with that? There are two ways you can do your time, new fish, A) do what the fuck I say when I say and fly under the radar, or B) you can do what you want and find your time here being hell on earth."

I went with option A and started taking off my clothes like everyone else. I never in a million years thought I'd be stripped of my dignity. There I was, standing butt ass naked, right behind a fat, sloppy, hairy-backed naked man. What made matters worse, I could feel the man behind me breathing, and knowing he was naked didn't sit well with my manhood.

We all stood there waiting for our turn to go through the diagnostic process. During the process, they shaved your head against the grain, so everyone knows you're the new fish. After that, they make you shower, and then they throw this powder on you. Finally, you are handed a set of off-white prison clothes and a pair of dingy boxers that have clearly been overworn. This beginning process alone made me never want to return to prison. *This will be my first and last time ever going to prison,* I promised myself.

## *Ch. 13 Chains and Choices:*

*"My brethren, count it all joy when you fall into various trials, knowing that the testing of your faith produces patience. But let patience have its perfect work, that you may be perfect and complete, lacking nothing."*
**–James 1:2-4 NKJV—**

The first 3 months, I sat back and observed everything, unsure how I wanted to spend my time. I didn't know whether to show I was a strong believer in Jesus Christ and go the "Jailhouse religious" route or just thug it out and roll with the Crips. That's how it's always been my whole life. I always believed in God, but I worried people would think I was weak. So, I lived the street life while the Holy Spirit inside me begged me to reconsider. My mother always taught me that when God is trying to get your attention, He will. However, it's up to you to listen, and I wasn't quite ready to listen.

It didn't take me long to learn the ropes of prison life. There might be 8 toilets, but you need to know which one is for number 1 and which is for number 2. One of the biggest inmate rules, besides never letting a man call you a bitch nor treating you like one, is that one TV stays on sports and the other on the news. I hated the news, so I always chose to watch whatever was on the sports channel.

When you first get into the dorm, the inmates ask what city you're from. Not only does that become your nickname, but they also point you toward the other inmates from your city. Me being from Fort Worth was a good thing because some of the most infamous criminals were from the Dallas/Fort Worth Metroplex. So that automatically helped get a little bit of respect; the rest had to be earned.

I quickly learned why they called this unit Butt Naked Gurney. Every time we were escorted out of our pod, a Correctional Officer would pull someone to the middle of the bowling alley and make them strip butt naked in front of everyone. The bowling alley was marked with yellow lines to help inmates find their way. The best way to avoid being pulled into the middle was to avoid eye contact with them so they wouldn't choose you, but sometimes that didn't even work.

"Shephard!", the CO called out. "Visit."

I was ecstatic because this was my first contact visit. Everyone was required to wait 90 days before their first visit, and mine just so happened to land on my birthday. Instead of spending my 21st birthday in Vegas as planned, I was spending it in prison.

I pulled out my pressed icy whites, which I had been holding onto for this moment. Most of the inmate jumpsuits were very dingy from being recycled over and over. Icy whites were brand-new jumpsuits that only laundry workers had access to. In prison, the saying "it's not what you know, it's who you know" really meant your livelihood. In my case, I connected with an old-school cat named Carl from Fort Worth. He was well respected throughout the prison, probably because he was serving a life sentence.

He wasn't a part of a gang or associated with anyone who did. He told me I reminded him of his son, so he looked out for me. Every Sunday, he'd encourage me to come to church and leave this gang activity alone.

Once you learn the ropes, you realize that inmates are running the prison. We were all assigned jobs, and your job became your hustle. Nothing was free; everyone had to contribute something to get something. If someone worked in the laundry, they could get you brand-new socks, drawers, and jumpsuits. If you wanted them pressed, they could even do that for an extra fee. If someone worked in the kitchen, they could get you fresh garlic, chicken, cakes, even knives, or anything else you would want from the kitchen. If someone worked for the cleaning crew, they could get you cleaning supplies like bleach, and because of their free mobility throughout the dorms, they could distribute whatever you needed to someone in another pod. The worst job was the Hoe Squad. If you've ever seen an old prison movie like "Life," you have an idea what it was like. The only way to avoid being on the Hoe Squad was to have a documented medical or mental health condition. I don't think I've ever been happier to suffer from major depression, because it meant I got to avoid being out in the hot sun every day, plowing the ground for hours.

As I walked down the bowling alley toward the visitation area, I began to feel overwhelmed with joy. I couldn't wait to see who all came to visit me. I stopped at the guarded gate and waited to be buzzed in. As soon as I walked inside, all my joy went out the window.

"Strip naked, take everything off, turn your socks inside out, and then throw them by your shoes. After that, turn around, spread your cheeks, bend over, and cough!" the CO demanded.

"Spread my cheeks?" I asked, confused.

"If you want to see whoever the hell drove all this way to see you, then I suggest you do what I say," he barked. Once again, my dignity was violated as I bent over and coughed. "Good! Now get dressed, sweet cheeks," the CO said.

My anger began to boil. I swear to God, if he were an inmate, I'd line that shit up quick and beat his ass. I got dressed and walked out to the visitation area, now pissed off. I quickly spotted my mother and Tam waiting for me.

"Happy birthday!" they both said in unison.

"Thank you."

"What's wrong?" my mother quickly asked, concerned, reading my facial expressions.

"These MFs have been making me do strip searches so many times since I got here. The CO back there just made me strip down, bend over, and cough," I said as I released my mother from my tightly squeezed hug.

"You're joking, right?" my mother asked in disbelief.

"I wish, but they don't call this Butt Naked Gurney for no reason," I responded as I hugged Tam and rubbed her stomach.

Tam was 5 months pregnant and definitely showing. I hugged and kissed Zion, who had just turned 1 in February. Then we all sat on the assigned side of the table.

I looked around and saw some familiar faces from the rec yard. The visitation room wasn't as big as I expected. Each inmate had a small square table with two chairs on one side and one on the other. You get one hug; other than that, no touching, which defeats the purpose of a contact visit.

"How are you? I miss you so much," I told Tam. It was something about being locked up that made me sentimental toward her.

"I'm doing well, but your daughter is working my nerves already. She's definitely going to have lots of hair because my heartburn is through the roof. Zion had his birthday, but enough about us. How are you? How is everyone treating you?" Tam asked, concerned.

"I am good. I wish I could take my shirt off and flex for y'all one time," I joked. "Naw, but for real, I am doing okay. I've been sitting back and learning the routine of this prison life. I work in the kitchen washing dishes, which is better than working the Hoe Squad. I can't believe something like that still exists. Every time I see them, I think of slavery. Other than that, I've been working out and staying out of the way."

"Have you run into anyone you know?" my mother asked.

"Yeah, J Dunn is here. Quay Quay's cousin Fat Fat is also here, and some other guys I know from the city, but none of them are in my dorm," I answered.

"Did you get the money I sent you and the letter?" Tam asked.

"Yes, thank you, and thank you too, mom. I know y'all can't afford to keep doing this, so I will be smart with the money. I hustle for things like chicken and onions or garlic from time to time, so I'm good. How's everyone else, though?" I asked, concerned.

"Jay is blowing up around the city with his new music and videos. Toni is doing well and still lives with Jay. Mani is doing well; there's a chance she might graduate early if she stays on course. She's taking extra credit classes her freshman year, so pray for her. Jeremiah is doing well, too, and should graduate next year. He's doing well in school, too. Cece is doing well, too. She misses you and told me to tell you she loves you," my mother said.

"Tell her I love her, too. I am glad to hear everyone is doing well. I miss y'all so much.

"Are you still reading your Bible?" Tam asked.

"Not as much as before, but every now and then I do. My Crip homies tell me I wasn't reading the Bible in the free world, so why come here being fake? I mean, in a way, I think they have a point. I feel like it's a slap in God's face that I only come to him when I am in need," I confessed.

"That is the dumbest thing I have ever heard. God comes to you at your weakest point in life, and He uses that for your testimony. If you were going the wrong way on the highway, wouldn't you turn around, or would you expect to find your destination in the midst of chaos? Draw closer to him, son. He has all the answers you've been looking for. He didn't bless you with 3 years for nothing. Open your eyes and ears and listen to what He has to say. Wake up and thank Him for waking you up, because Today is never promised. Who cares what other inmates think! Did I teach you to be a follower or a leader?" my mother asked.

"A leader, I answered.

"So, be a leader and continue to draw closer to God. None of these inmates will be with you when you're answering to God. I'd hate for you to miss out on everything He specifically has in store for you because you followed the misguided direction of your crip homies," my mother added.

"You're right, Mom, but this is the pen! If I'm seen as weak, they'll treat me like a B word," I said, not cursing out of respect for my mother.

"Matthew 5:10, Blessed are those who are persecuted for righteousness' sake: for theirs is the kingdom of heaven. It also says that His sheep hear My voice, and I know them, and they follow Me. Read your Bible, son, and learn how they treated Jesus. This world is not our home; we are foreigners, just waiting to be called home, the Bible says. Choose this day whom you will serve!"

"Where is all this coming from, Mom? I mean, you always had us in church, but this side of you is different," I asked, noticing a change in my mother.

"I am becoming a minister for our church," my mother answered.

"Wow! I love that, but why a minister?" I asked.

"Honestly, I didn't want to be a minister, but I knew that was God's calling for my life. If I didn't obey, I'd be like Jonah or worse; He'd use my death for His ministry."

"Wow," was all I could say as my mother's words impacted me.

"I am getting ordained next month," she added.

"Congratulations. I am proud of you," I told her.

"Yeah, she's been an inspiration to us all," Tam chimed in, looking around. "What is it like in here?"

"It's very racist in here and segregated, from the inmates to the guards. You have to know who you can talk to or eat with. It's so racist that you have to get the okay to fight another race because you might start a riot. I hate it because, being light-skinned, I get crap from everyone. I tried using Magic Cream to shave one time, and it burned my face. This CO told me, "You thought you were black enough to use that, huh?" I couldn't believe it. I don't get bullied or anything; it's just jokes from everyone. Besides that, I hate the layout the most. I don't know who designed these dorms, but the TVs are mounted above the showers, which causes a lot of fights. Nobody wants to see naked men, but with no curtains on the showers, we're forced to see a glimpse while we watch sports or get our daily news. Since the security booth is at the center of all four pods, if any fights do break out, they are quickly de-escalated. That's just the showers; the toilet situation is far worse. If more than 2 people have to take a dump at the same time, then that third or fourth person will find themselves "knee knocking" with the guy next to them."

"Knee knocking?" My mother and Tam asked in unison.

"Knee knocking is where you're literally touching knees with the person pooping next to you; smelling all their stank."

"Eww!" Tam said. "Well, thankfully, you don't have that long," Tam encouraged.

We sat there talking and laughing. Since my mother drove so far, we were blessed to get a special contact visit, which meant a 2-hour visit instead of a normal 1-hour visit.

My heart was filled with joy, but I started to feel myself getting sad because the visit made me want to go home with my family.

"Time's up, Mr. Shephard," a CO informed me.

I got up and hugged my family goodbye, saying, "I love y'all."

"Love you too," they responded before turning around and leaving. To my surprise, I had to go through the butt-naked, bend-over, and cough procedure all over again before being escorted back to my pod.

*God, when I get out, I promise never to return to prison again! I miss my family so much. Please help me get back to them. I don't want to be here anymore!* I begged inside as I climbed onto my bunk, threw my blanket over my head, and cried myself to sleep.

The next morning, I was working in the kitchen and got promoted from dishwasher to line cook. I didn't like it because the inmates who had worked there longer made me do all the grunt work.

One guy named Juan was the worst; he was the head chef and known for bossing people around. I guess today was my day because every time a can needed to be opened, he would say something in Spanish and then tell me to do it. I didn't know what he said, but I didn't like the vibe I was getting."

"Come take these pancakes off and put them in the pan," Juan directed after telling me to open the cans of green beans.

Man, why the hell can't you do it? I thought. I went over to take the pancakes off, and he chuckled, saying something in Spanish to his friend. I felt like I was being tested, so when I went back to opening cans of pears. He called for me again, but this time I ignored him.

"Hey, you don't hear me talking to you," Juan said. "Come get these pancakes as I said, or else."

"Na bruh, you got it," I replied, unbothered by the threat.

"What did you say?" he said, approaching me.

"Oh, you can speak English now," I said, adding fuel to the fire.

"I can't stand you lazy black motherfuckers. Man, you're a bitch!" he said, flexing his chest.

"Let me look at that shit!" was prison slang for let's fight.

We walked to the back alone as everyone else pretended to work. As soon as we got there, he quickly swung at me. I weaved the wild punch, and he quickly grabbed me. My adrenaline shot through the roof as I knocked his arm down and swung as hard as I could, connecting to his jaw. After finding success, I hit him with a quick jab followed by another haymaker. Juan stumbled back, then rushed me, hitting me with the quickest three-punch combo I've ever seen. The first was to my rib, the second to my upper torso, and the last connected to my right eye. He then grabbed me and attempted to throw me to the ground, but I refused. I broke free from his grip and grabbed his head, kneeing his face as hard as I could. Out of nowhere, the riot squad came in and tackled me to the ground before putting handcuffs on me.

I spent the next 60 days in segregation, aka "the pits of hell." I couldn't believe it was 2011, yet there were still places in Texas without air conditioning. The tiny cells made it very hot and humid. The only relief came from a small hole that blew lukewarm air, much like the A/C in a car when you first start it. The heat was so bad that it made you sweat in your sleep. Which would soak the mattress; making you feel like you wet the bed. What made things worse was that the only time you left the cell was during the 1-hour yard time you received, if the CO felt like it that day. I spent my whole time praying because I honestly didn't know if I would survive 60 days. After all, it wasn't even the peak of summer yet.

When they finally let me out, I promised myself I would never go back, no matter what, at least not in the summer. When I returned to the regular population, I had a small reputation from my fight in the kitchen. Everyone showed me respect, and I was somewhat comfortable in a place where I had no business getting comfortable. I was gambling in sports, on the Knock table, in chess; 1 could say I had my hands in all the wrong things.

The most challenging aspect of incarceration isn't the physical confinement within the cell walls, but rather the emotional separation from family and friends outside. I was hearing all kinds of crazy stories, and the hardest part was that I couldn't do anything. I heard about Spencer's fight at Club Chrome and his gun charge, which resulted in him getting 6 years TDC.

I also heard that my best friend, Jessica, had started dialysis due to kidney problems. I was truly heartbroken because Jessica had already been through so much, from the death of her son's father to becoming a single mother. I couldn't imagine what she was going through, mentally or physically. It felt like I was being forced to be a bystander in my friends' and family's lives.

I remember getting the letter about my friend Bob, who was critically injured after being hit by a car. I was told he was fighting for his life. After reading that, I felt myself sinking back into my bunk—trying to hide my pain from the others in my pod. A flashback of our meeting in the 3rd grade came to mind. We were in Mrs. Hunter's class and were supposed to present our knock-knock joke. I knew for sure I had the best one; after all, I was the class comedian even back then.

"Knock knock?"

"Who's there?" the class questioned.

"Yo," I answered.

"Yo, who?"

"Yo mama! Now, open the damn door!" I replied, giggling, as the class burst out laughing. Mrs. Hunter was not amused and forced me to sit next to her. Then comes good ole Bob, right on cue.

"Knock knock."

"Who's there?" the class asked

"Yo!" he replied, snickering.

"You better not repeat what Mr. Shephard said!" Mrs. Hunter interrupted.

"I'm not," he said slyly.

"Okay, go on," she said

"Knock knock!" he started over

"Who's there?"

"Yo!" he replied.

"Yo, who?"

"Yo, Daddy! Now open this damn door like yo mama said."

I laughed at the memory; ever since then, we became close friends. So, the reality of him fighting for his life instantly made me sad; not only for him but also for his family. I prayed for Bob's recovery, for his family and mine.

Letter after letter, I kept receiving bad news. It made my time extremely hard because, no matter how much I wanted to do something, I was constantly reminded that I was shackled. One day, I was called to the mailroom to sign a legal document. When I got there, I opened a legal notice from Child Protective Services. It informed me that the state was taking custody of my son, Patrick, due to child neglect and endangerment. Word travels fast from the free world to inside the prison walls. I had already received news that his mother was being abused; but refused to leave. Now, CPS took all her kids. I immediately got angry and hurt because once again, there was nothing I could do. I then didn't want to imagine my four-year-old being taken away from his mother.

*God, please protect my son Patrick. Also, Lord, I know You want better for me, but I can't be seen as weak in here. I see how these inmates treat the Bible freaks. So, please just protect me. That's all I ask.*

Just like that, I made up my mind to go my way and hope God would protect me, but like my mother always said, a hard head makes a soft behind, like Jonah.

The date was May 28th, 2011, and my Crip homies and I were busting a spread for my right-hand man, Zion. Although they didn't know him personally, they still showed their respect for one of our city's fallen soldiers. This marked Zion's second death anniversary, but it still felt like yesterday. Even though I was hurting inside, I couldn't show it.

I was thankful for Carl; the one person I could keep it real with. I told him how I wanted to separate myself from this thug lifestyle and live for Christ. I told him how I felt I'd be viewed as weak, but also how the death of Zion has affected my life. He didn't judge me, but simply poured his wisdom and knowledge into me. Although he didn't engage in any gang activity, he made a cake out of a pack of cookies for Zion. I was amazed at how creative the inmates were.

"Yo, I want to thank y'all for this," I told the homies. Before they could respond, a CO walked into our pod.

"Shephard!" the CO called out.

"What's up, Boss?" I asked.

"You're being called down to the chaplain's office," he said.

"For what?" I asked, curiously.

"You can ask him when you get there. Now hurry up!"

I got up and put my jumpsuit on over my commissary shirt and shorts. When I was ready to go, the guard escorted me out of the pod and toward the bowling alley that led to the prison's church. As we walked, my mind was racing. *Why would the chaplain want to speak with me?* I wondered. I'd never been inside the prison's church before, but passing by the singing always called out to my soul.

We continued down the bowling alley to the other side of the prison, where the church was located. A cool breeze blew from the night sky as the stars gleamed back at me. The calm night gave me a sense of peace. Being trapped in the hot dorm all day made me appreciate cool nights like these.

When we finally reached the chaplain's office, the CO walked me inside and ordered me to have a seat. I sat in the chair in front of the chaplain's desk. A couple of minutes later, a man walked in, and I knew it was the chaplain because he looked like your average youth pastor.

"Why did you want to speak with me?" I asked as he sat across from me. He finally looked up, and that's when I noticed he had been crying. Wait, what's going on? Why would the chaplain be crying? Something isn't right. I wasn't sure what, but I could feel something was wrong.

"Mr. Shephard, this is the part of my job that I dislike the most. I wish we were meeting on better terms, but I am the chaplain, James Peters. You can call me James," he started, confirming something wasn't right. "Before I explain to you why you're here, I need you to promise me you'll control yourself."

Why did this feel like déjà vu? "I promise," I answered. He then picked up the phone receiver and pressed a flashing button.

"Hello, yes ma'am, he is right here, one second," Chaplain Peters said. Ma'am? Who is he talking to? I thought. "Remember your promise, please," he said as he gave me the phone.

"Hello," I said nervously.

"Hello, my baby," my mother said, crying.

"Mom, what's wrong?" I asked, realizing something had to be wrong if they were allowing her to contact me through the chaplain's office. The memory of the last phone call like this settled in my stomach as I prepared for what was to come.

"Baby, your brother Toni was shot, and he is in the ICU," my mother said, bawling. My heart stopped. No, Lord, not my brother! I already lost one person close to me; please do not let me lose another. I took the phone away from my ear as I could no longer keep my composure. All the pain I've been dealing with since Zion's death, now mixed with my brother, was too much to bear. Lord, what do You want from me?

I picked the phone back up and asked between sobs, "Who…shot…him?"

"It was Manny" …

## *Ch. 14 Faith In The Fire:*

*"See, I am doing a new thing! Now it springs up; do you not perceive it? I am making a way in the wilderness and streams in the wasteland."*

**—Isaiah 43:19 –**

"I feel… so far… from You, Lord, but I still hear You calling me! Those simple things I once knew are drawing me. I must confess, Lord, I've been blessed… yet my soul is not satisfied… Renew my faith… restore my joy… and, Lord, will You dry my weeping eyes. Sing it, church," the lead singer sang.

"Take me back…" everyone sang from the depths of their souls.

"I wanna go back…" the lead singer sang, ad-libs.

"Take me back, dear Lord… to the place where I first received You."

I listened to the souls cry out in unison; it gave the lyrics a deeper impact on my heart. I stood there with my eyes closed, listening to a song I'd never heard. I don't know whether it was the powerful lyrics, a group of men pouring out their hearts to God, or the lead singer's angelic voice, but the Holy Spirit within me stirred as my hands went up in surrender to the Lord.

"Lord, I prayed for Zion, and it didn't quite turn out as I expected. I can't go through the same thing with my brother Toni. Please help him pull through, Lord, I beg You. I am ready to listen to what You have to say, Lord. Speak to me, Lord, and I will listen. Teach me, Father, and I will learn," I poured my heart out to God.

It was my first time going to church, and after the news I had just received, it was the only place I wanted to be. I felt it deep down—I knew God was trying to get my attention, and for the first time, I was ready to listen. My mom always said that God works in mysterious ways, but that day, those words finally took on a new meaning. The voice that sounded almost angelic was Carl's. Here was a man serving a life sentence, yet he was pouring

162

his heart to God with complete humility and faith. I once thought he was respected simply because of the time he was serving, but now I understand it was something far greater. In that moment, everything became clear. I finally understood why he had wanted me to come to church so badly—and why I was meant to be there.

The next song he sang, I had never heard before, but I knew I'd never forget the words or how he sang them.

"Tomorrow is… a brand-new day… and all my sins… have been washed away! My hands look new… my lives complete and by his blood … I have been redeemed, oh yes… we are…. more than conquerors…oh yes; we are. I've seen His face… I've touched His hands… and finally… now I understand… why He saved a wretch … a wretch like me."

I closed my eyes and listened to him sing as I surrendered to God. My heart was heavy, and I could no longer carry these burdens alone. My mother always told me to give my problems to God; the only problem was that I didn't know how.

After church, I returned to my dorm just in time for mail call. When the guard called my name, I ran to him, anxious to see how Toni was. I grabbed the J pay letter from my mother and quickly read it.

*Dear Son,*

*I am so sorry to bring you such sad news in a place where I cannot comfort you. Everything happened so fast, and yet it felt terrifyingly slow. One minute, we were hearing medical terms we barely understood, and the next, we were watching doctors rush with urgency… this made our hearts sink. The decision to put your brother on a helicopter wasn't just quick—it was desperate. As the blades lifted him into the sky toward the main hospital in downtown Fort Worth, it felt like we were watching his last chance disappear into the air. All we could do was pray—pray that he would make it, pray that we wouldn't get the call we were dreading. Those moments were filled with fear, hope, and helplessness all at once. And then, against what felt like impossible odds, he survived. Because of the doctors' swift, decisive actions, your brother was given his life back—and we were given a miracle. Please get your life right with God, son. Tomorrow is never promised! I love you so much, son! I'll come to see you when I can, but I put money on your books.*

*Love mom, Love you, Infinity!*

I was finally ready to give my life to God behind prison walls, but it didn't happen overnight. It wasn't dramatic at first; no thunder, no sudden freedom—just a broken man who had finally run out of excuses. Ever since the news about my brother, I had been attending church services for weeks, sitting quietly, listening more than singing, watching more than participating. I still had a lot of things I was battling with mentally, and number one on the list was Manny. It's not like I could avoid him since he's the uncle to my son, so I made up my mind that I was going to get payback for my brother.

A couple of months later, I finally received some good news. The warden figured that, after the bad news I received, hearing some good news would help me mentally. I got called back down to the chaplain's office, but this time, the person on the other end wasn't my mother; it was my wife, with my newborn daughter crying in the background.

"Say hey, daddy," Tam said clearly, still in pain but more concerned about the moment.

"Hey, daddy's baby," I said with so much joy. "How are my girls?"

"I am in pain, but I am okay. Ana is good too. She is so beautiful, head full of hair," Tam said proudly.

The chaplain allowed us to talk for only 10 minutes, but it was the best 10 minutes of my sentence. I felt seen again and was floating on cloud 9.

Later that day, they were offering baptism at church, and I thought it was a sign from God. As I entered the water, my wrists were free of shackles, but the heaviness on my soul remained—yet I felt an indescribable sense of release. For the first time in my life, I wasn't pretending. I wasn't bargaining. I was surrendering. I wasn't asking God to get me out of prison anymore; I was asking Him to get prison out of me. Not long after that, everything shifted.

The tension in the pods was thick the next day. You could feel it before you ever heard it. Whispers traveled across the unit. Everyone was alert. Shoes were laced tighter — not for comfort, but for war. When you've been locked up long enough, you learn to read the signs. A riot was looming.

It started in A-Pod. What began as a commissary dispute quickly turned into a full-blown race riot. Through the large glass windows separating the pods, I watched chaos explode. Men swung locks tied to belts like weapons. Bodies slammed into bunks. Blood splattered onto the concrete. The sound was unreal. Metal clanging, men screaming, alarms blaring over everything; my heart was racing so fast I could feel it in my throat.

Then it spread. D-Pod erupted next and the tension soon shifted toward us. I watched white inmates group together, forming a wall. My homies did the same. There was no room for hesitation. If you didn't stand, you'd be marked later. If you did, you might not walk away.

Fear took over. I hopped off my bunk, took a deep breath, and prayed silently:

*Lord, please protect me. I don't want this life anymore.*

Three of the four pods were fighting now. I could see blood through the windows. Men falling. Men screaming. It felt like the whole dorm was about to explode. As both sides started moving toward each other in our pod, a man stepped between us.

It was Carl. The same man who sang in church with a voice that sounded like heaven had cracked through concrete. Shirt off. Arms stretched wide. No fear in his eyes.

"WE WILL NOT HAVE THIS IN THIS DORM!" he shouted. "IN JESUS' NAME, I REBUKE SATAN OUT OF HERE. IF ANYONE WANTS TO FIGHT, YOU'LL HAVE TO GO THROUGH ME AND GOD!"

Time froze. Then, to my disbelief, the men backed down, one by one. The riot alarm sounded. Guards rushed in, screaming for everyone to back up. I stood there stunned. I had never seen faith look like that. Not weak. Not quiet; unshakeable. That moment changed me.

After the riot, they broke up the entire dorm. I was transferred to the Dawson Unit in downtown Dallas. Inmates called it Club Dawson due to the A/C, cable TV, and radios. I was excited. That excitement vanished the moment I walked into my new pod. Scriptures covered the walls, crosses were everywhere, and the TVs were off. The men were reading Bibles, and instead of mugging me, they greeted me with, "God bless you, brother."

At first, I didn't know what to think. Prison had trained me to stay guarded, but this place felt different — like I had stepped into a refuge God built inside chaos. I quickly learned I was in a faith-based dorm. I found out that every morning started with praise and worship after breakfast, then hours of uninterrupted Bible study. No TVs until after five. No distractions like dominoes, spades, or knock. No gambling and basically no fun. I wanted to leave but knew I needed to stay. That clarity saved my life.

At first, I hated not having access to TV, but over time, the quiet became healing. What had the greatest impact were the one-on-one Bible studies. My mother told me that sometimes God places people in your life to be a guardian angel. Well, Paul was that for me. He was an accountant who didn't quite cross all his T's and dot all his I's, if you know what I mean. He was charged with a white-collar crime and decided to teach others about Christ while incarcerated.

Paul became a mentor and constantly challenged me. He stimulated my brain, which helped me grow and learn. We read the Bible, highlighting the five W's as we went. I began learning who wrote what and why. It was cool learning about Paul in the Bible and how he went from killing Christians to bringing people to Christ. He also wrote most of the New Testament. Learning about Job first made me upset. I didn't understand why he went through so much, but Paul helped me understand that our thoughts aren't His thoughts nor our ways His ways. He showed me that God knows every hair on our heads. I then thought maybe God knew Job wouldn't curse Him and trusted Job with that battle. Due to Job's faithfulness, God blessed him tenfold.

Here I was learning from men who were serving decades in prison. Not only did they teach me patience, but these former gang leaders taught me humility. Brothers who had lost everything taught me forgiveness. They didn't just quote Scripture — they lived it.

"Be still and know that I am God," Paul recited. "Do not be consumed by the world, but be transformed by the renewing of your mind." Those verses stopped being words and became instructions as Paul continued to pour into me.

As crazy as it might sound, prison became the best-worst thing to happen to me. Being in the faith-based dorm no longer felt like prison but instead as if I was at a retreat with God. He was slowly healing my broken heart from the Zion incident. Not only was I changing, but I also found reading entertaining and soothing. I must have read 1000 books, from Nicholas Sparks to Sistah Souljah, James Patterson, Eric Jerome Dickey, and Ashley & JaQuavis. I was even reading self-help books like Mentor: The Kid & The Ceo by Tom Pace with Walter Jenkins. It was when I read The Purpose Driven Life by Rick Warren that I learned God's calling for my life. After reading many urban fiction stories, including Midnight, my favorite by Sistah Souljah, I knew my real-life story was worth sharing. I immediately started writing as much about my life as I could remember. After I wrote 4 chapters, I asked Paul to edit them because he informed me of his Bachelor's degree in English.

To be honest, I didn't want to get out of prison. I wanted to stay in the faith-based dorm so I could finish my book and build my faith.  However, I was unaware that God wasn't done with my story quite yet. One night during Bible study, a group of new guards came through on an orientation tour. One female guard stopped and listened longer than the others. She asked a question about fear and purpose, which she mentioned she was struggling with personally. I understood her feelings, since I also grew up in the church but had also been afraid to live boldly for God. Suddenly, numerous scriptures flooded my mind as she spoke.

Paul looked at me as he must have seen my excitement, because he said, "Andre, would you like to answer that?"

Without hesitation, scriptures poured out of me:

"Ephesians 3:12 In whom we have boldness and access with confidence by the faith of Him. Hebrews 4:16 Let us therefore come boldly unto the throne of grace. 2nd Timothy 3:12 Yea, and all that will live godly in Christ Jesus shall suffer persecution. John 20:29 Blessed are those who have not seen and yet have believed. God has not given us a spirit of fear, but of power, love, and a sound mind." —2 Timothy 1:7

After I explained the scriptures to her and shared my testimony, I asked if I could pray over her. To my surprise, she agreed and we prayed together right there. I watched her break down in tears, thanking God. I will never forget the feeling God gave me that night. Chills would be an understatement. It felt like God woke my spirit up! It was the greatest feeling I've ever felt.

That was the moment I realized God was never punishing me—He was always molding me to be of use for His glory.

After serving two years and 3 months, I finally came up for parole. Part of me didn't want to leave because I was closer to God than ever before. On the other hand, I was also afraid of all the temptations the devil was ready to throw at me. The biggest test was what I'd do to Manny if we ever crossed paths. Paul taught me that we must forgive others, because if we don't, how can we expect God to forgive us?  But this was personal. Manny ruined my life and the anger I still felt, made me realize I had more work to do in this faith-based dorm. If I was released now, I'd be placed in the center of the highway with oncoming traffic, instead of on the access road, which would allow me enough time to gain speed and momentum. I would be bound to crash.

After my parole hearing, I received an F-I-6, which meant I'd have to complete a 6-month program before my release. I was frustrated because I wanted an F-I-1, which would have allowed me to go home in 30 days. I would only have 3 months of parole, so it was pointless waste of time.

God had many tests waiting for me when I left the faith-based dorm, as I feared. After reading and studying the Bible, I knew the devil would attack as soon as he could.

At first, I was angry about being released in 6 months instead of 30 days, but God knew what I didn't. Paul said to be happy that I was going home early at all, and it made me feel selfish for complaining about something other inmates yearned for. He also told me that maybe God had bigger plans for me, and that was exactly right. My first test came when I was transferred to a pre-release unit called The Hamilton. I ran into a friend I had known since middle school, named K.C. Due to his size and strength, other inmates in the tank were afraid of him. I realized God wanted to test me around old friends. So, my next 6 months I taught K.C. what I had learned in the Bible. Some people knew him as a Crip, but I knew his heart, and he loved God. We would work out our minds, bodies, and souls every day. Scriptures and spreads were our thing. It made time fly as we reminisced about the old times.

My next test was the biggest one that I wasn't ready for. When I finally got released, my mother was right there to pick me up. I hugged her with so much joy as we cried in the prison parking lot. She held me tightly, refusing to let me go. I missed her so much and was thankful for her being there every step of the way. I let go and turned, looking for my wife, but to my surprise, she wasn't there. However, my two childhood friends, Al and Ant, were there.

I first met Al when we were four years old. We went to pre-K together and lived in the same apartment complex. Ant was his little brother. Al and I became best buddies almost instantly. That lasted until one unforgettable day. I saw a group of guys messing with my crush, laughing as they threw her shoe over a gated fence. Trying to be a hero, I reached through the gate to grab it— completely unaware that the gate was opening to let a car through. I was so focused on winning her heart that I didn't notice the danger until it was too late. The gate slammed into me, trapping me in between. My foot twisted all the way to the right, got stuck and pinned.

My grandfather came running out of the house and rushed me to the hospital. The doctors said I was lucky—it was a bad sprain. I was on bed rest for a couple of weeks. When I finally stepped outside again, the first thing I saw was Al and my crush… holding hands.I confronted him immediately. His mom made him come inside, but right before he walked away, I sucker-punched him in the eye and ran home as fast as I could. As I took off, he screamed out the window, "I hate you, Andre!"

Somehow, after all that, we've been best friends ever since. So, seeing them there—welcoming me home meant more than I could ever put into words. I know that everyone isn't as blessed to have their childhood friends still standing by their side. What really struck me, was this new mature version of Ant. He had grown into his own, yet he was still my little brother in spirit. I had watched him follow a path that could have led him straight into trouble, just like me, but I knew I had to share some wisdom with him, before it was too late. Judging by the way he was living now, I could see he listened.

"Wassup, bro," I said, pulling Al into a hug.

"What's up? You good?" he asked.

"I'm better now," I replied.

"My boy!" I shouted as I hugged Ant.

"What's good, big bro?" he said, returning the embrace.

"Man, you tell me? Looks like someone's been paying attention," I said, nodding at his confident stride and fresh drip.

"You know me," he said confidently, as a small laugh slipped out. "Mama and Pops wanna see you and the little sisters."

"Of course, but let's go see them after I go home and shower. I need to get out of these clothes ASAP," I said.

"Okay, we'll follow," Al said.

On the ride to my mother's house, she dropped the news that Tam was in Mississippi. My heart sank. I wasn't just missing her; I was missing my daughter and this was my first chance to hold her in years. I wanted that feeling of being missed and desired—the same type of love I'd seen my mom give Manny every time he came home from prison, but that wasn't my story today. Still, I was surrounded by family and friends pouring love into me, and that helped.

Once I got changed, the first stop was to Dre Dre's school. When he saw me, he ran straight into my arms, crying. My twin, my firstborn, was finally in my arms. I missed him more than words could say. Before I went to prison, he lived with me. During my time away, he stayed with my mother, giving him stability while I lost mine. Holding him again felt like a piece of my soul had been returned.

When Tam finally returned a few days later, despite the three years gone, our reunion was quiet but electric. I didn't question her or the past; I just knew I had to start fresh as a husband and father. My daughter clung to me immediately; tiny arms wrapped around my neck. That night, I slept holding her, savoring the long-held dream finally realized. Zion was walking and talking, and though I wasn't his biological father, being his guide and protector felt right.

Tam noticed the change in me immediately. She fell in love again—not just with me, but with the new version of me that had survived, grown, and vowed to be better. Things were going great, but then came the shock.

A couple of weeks later, she told me she thought she was pregnant. When the test confirmed it, joy shot through me. I was determined to do right this time and care for her, Ana'kele, Zion and our new baby. By the third month, we finally found an OBGYN she liked after a frustrating search. My gut twisted over some of her reasons for rejecting the others, but I pushed the feeling aside, relieved the search was over. Excitement was high as my mother drove us to the appointment, equally excited to learn about her newest grandchild on the horizon.

Tam filled out the paperwork while I waited, my heart thrumming with anticipation. When we were called in, I tried to keep my excitement in check.

"I bet it's a boy. Kele's gonna be my only girl, watch," I said, hugging Tam.

"Nah, I feel it's a girl. Heartburn doesn't lie," she teased.

We laughed nervously, hearts full of hope. Then Dr. Andrews entered with a bright smile and a confident aura.

"Hello, I'm Dr. Andrews," she said.

I introduced us, proud and protective: "I'm Andre Shephard Jr., this is my beautiful wife, Tam, and my mother, Faith."

After pleasantries were exchanged, she got down to business.

"How far along are you, Tam?"

"Three months," Tam answered.

"Good. We'll do a sonogram today to check the baby's health and growth. We'll also measure the head, and I'll just take a few notes to make sure everything's right," she explained.

I held my breath as she applied the gel and the band, the room filling with the rhythmic sound of a heartbeat.

"Oh my God," I whispered, tears welling. Three months ago, I was in prison. Now here I was, holding my family, hearing my child's heartbeat. I thought, *thank You God.*

And then…

"Hmmm," Dr. Andrews murmured.

My heart froze. *Hmmm? What does that mean?*

"Hmmm," she said again.

"Is something wrong?" my mother asked, her voice tight with concern.

"Before I say anything, Mrs. Shephard, you have the right to discuss this privately," the doctor said.

I stepped forward, firm. "I'm her husband, and this is my child. Tell me whatever it is."

Tam gave a small nod, eyes steady. "It's okay, Andre. You're part of this."

Dr. Andrews took a deep breath. "Good news first, you're having a boy. But there's more—according to the size of the baby's head and body, you're further along than you think. The measurements put you at the end of your fifth month—approaching your third trimester."

Time stopped. My mind scrambled. Five months? I was in prison five months ago. Could this be… impossible?

"How sure are you?" I asked, trying to keep my voice steady, though a storm of disbelief and anger raged inside.

"Sir, I've been doing this for 15 years," she said softly. "I'm rarely wrong."

I looked at my mother, and her shock reflected my own. Tears ran down my face as feelings of rage, betrayal, and confusion overwhelmed me all at once. The old version of myself might have reacted violently, trembling and fists clenched, but I had changed. I simply couldn't go back to prison—not now, not EVER!

*Lord, how could this happen?* I thought, clutching the arms of the chair. My world had shattered in an instant.

"Sir… are you okay?" Dr. Andrews asked gently, reading the pain in my eyes.

"No," my mother whispered. "He just got out of prison four months ago."

## *Present Day:*

*"Children are a heritage from the Lord, offspring a reward from him. Like arrows in the hands of a warrior are children born in one's youth. Blessed is the man whose quiver is full of them."*

**—Psalm 127:3-5 (NIV)—**

My smile was bright, my heart full of happiness, and my soul at peace as I drove down the road with my wife beside me and a car filled with laughter behind us. The voices of seven children filled the space between the windows and the sky, each one a reminder of answered prayers, fought battles, and kept promises. With one more on the way, our family would soon be complete with nine children. What might seem like chaos, was actually filled with love. Years ago, I couldn't imagine peace like this. My past life felt like an endless storm, but now I was living in the calm that God had brought.

Her name was Miss Linda. From the moment she spoke, she reminded me of Miss Karolyn with a mix of my mother. She had that same gentle authority, the kind that doesn't demand attention but commands respect—a woman of God. You could feel it. She began talking with my wife, effortlessly quoting scripture—words that didn't feel rehearsed but lived-in, seasoned by time and faith. As she spoke, something stirred in me. A quiet knowing. The sense that this moment was not random. It felt God-sent.

When my wife introduced me, Miss Linda looked at us both, then glanced toward the children scattered around the park.

"Are these all y'all's children?" she asked.

I smiled, "Oh yes," I said. "We have nine combined."

Her eyes widened in pure amazement. "Nine?" she said, almost laughing in disbelief. "All from you?"

My wife chuckled, but then she shook her head.

"Uh…No… no, ma'am." Then I paused. "How much time do you have?"

She smiled and leaned back slightly. "Oh, I have all day. I love a good story."

I nodded, feeling the weight and beauty of the journey rise in my chest.

"Well then," I said, "let me tell you how these roads lead to A Shephard…"

## *To My Children:*

You are the reason I chose healing over hiding, growth over comfort, and truth over pride. Every page of this book was written with you in mind. I love you all more than my heart could ever articulate. I pray that my story reminds you that God's grace is stronger than your past mistakes. The sky is not the limit, you are! Be great, healed and free. This is for YOU!

*"For I know the plans I have for you," declares the Lord, "plans to prosper you and not to harm you, plans to give you hope and a future."*

**—Jeremiah 29:11 (NIV)—**

Andre' Shephard Jr. is an author, speaker, and college student whose life is a testament to redemption, faith, and transformation. From incarceration to education, his journey reflects what is possible when purpose replaces pain and faith meets obedience.

Often described as "from the pen to the pen," Andre's story breaks free from the penitentiary mindset, inspiring healing, hope, and change. He is a current student and soon-to-be graduate earning an Associate's degree in Business Administration—proving that restoration is not only spiritual but also practical.

Anchored in Philippians 1:6 — "He who has begun a good work in you will carry it on to completion until the day of Jesus Christ" — Andre speaks to those who feel disqualified by their past, reminding them that God is not finished and that purpose is still unfolding.